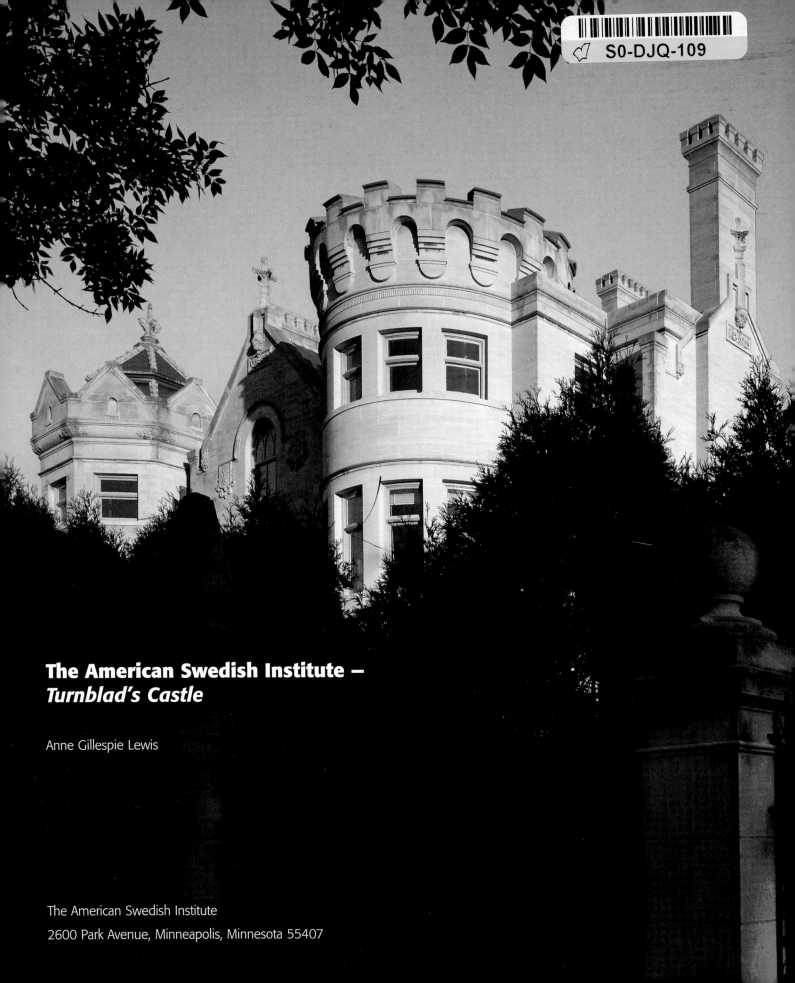

The American Swedish Institute –
Turnblad's Castle

Anne Gillespie Lewis

The American Swedish Institute

2600 Park Avenue, Minneapolis, Minnesota 55407

Library of Congress Cataloging-in-Publication Data

Lewis, Anne Gillespie
    The American Swedish Institute—Turnblad's Castle / Anne Gillespie Lewis.
        p. cm.
    English and Swedish.
        1. Mansions–Minnesota–Minneapolis. 2. Turnblad, Swan J., 1860-1933–Homes and
    haunts–Minnesota–Minneapolis. 3. American Swedish Institute (Minneapolis,
    Minn.)–History. 4. Minneapolis (Minn.)–Buildings, structures, etc. I. American
    Swedish Institute (Minneapolis, Minn.) II. Title.

    NA7511.4.M56 L49 1999
    728.8'09776'579–dc21

                                                            99-047672

Swedish Summary: Barbro Roehrdanz

Graphic Designer: Randy Urlacher

Printer: Ideal Printers, Inc.

ISBN 0-9674399-0-6

Dedication

This story of one Swedish immigrant is dedicated to the hundreds of thousands of Swedes who bravely set out for North America, to those they left behind, and to all their descendants.

Special Acknowledgement

This publication would not have been possible without the generous financial support of Barbro Sachs Osher, President of the Barbro Sachs Osher Pro Suecia Foundation, San Francisco, California.

Foreword

For nearly a century, Swan J. Turnblad's "castle," the 33-room mansion on the edge of downtown Minneapolis, in Minnesota, the most Swedish of all states, has fascinated the public. Built of sober gray Indiana limestone, it sits solidly inside its wrought iron fence, as quiet and seemingly inscrutable as the man who built it. But the man and his castle had another side, one that reached back to Swedish fairy tales and legends for inspiration and strength, dazzling lesser beings and buildings with the sheer magnitude of their achievements. Both the man and his castle had their detractors; some say Turnblad misled investors in his newspapers, others sniffed that the castle was a mish-mash of styles. But the naysayers are gone, and the castle remains, as does the memory of the man who first willed it into being and then gave it to the Swedish-American community as a cultural center for everyone to enjoy.

This is the story of Swan J. Turnblad and his castle. It is not a full biography, as that is beyond the scope of this book. However, curious readers will find many of their questions answered about the man behind the building and we hope they will judge him as gently as they should judge themselves. The house, a magnificent and exuberant melange of richly carved wood, beautifully molded plaster and graceful rooms, cannot be separated from the spirit of the man who had it built and we have kept them together in these pages.

Many people have contributed to this book. All of us who worked on the book owe a great debt to researcher and American Swedish Institute member Lawrence G. Hammerstrom. Valuable information about the automobiles owned by Turnblad was provided by Robert R. Johnson, also an American Swedish Institute member. Another member, William H. Nelson, led several of us over to the Zuhrah Shrine building. Archivist/Librarian Marita Karlisch, Communications Manager Jan McElfish, Bookstore Manager Annette Bittner, Curator Curt Pederson, Membership Coordinator Annette Lernvik-Djupström, Executive Secretary Sandra Schwamb and several members of the Sisters of St. Joseph, who served at the Academy of the Holy Angels in Richfield, Minnesota, were also wonderful resources and all patiently answered the many questions the author posed. Barbro Roehrdanz provided an excellent summary of the book for Swedish readers. A special thank you to Bruce Karstadt, Executive Director of the American Swedish Institute, for seeing the project through and always making time for the author's questions. A personal thanks from the author to her husband, Stephen Lewis, who offered his usual understanding and support during this long project. The writing of this book is only half of the effort, however; graphic artist/designer Randy Urlacher worked with the committee and the author from the first. We hope readers will enjoy the results of our efforts.

Anne Gillespie Lewis
Minneapolis, Minnesota, 1999.

Table of Contents

Cedar Avenue in Minneapolis, pictured around 1890, was in the midst of the Scandinavian immigrant community.

Cedar Avenue i Minneapolis, omkring 1890, låg mitt i de skandinaviska immigrant-kvarteren.

Swan J. Turnblad and His Castle

In 1929, just before the stock market crashed and the Great Depression began, Minneapolis, Minnesota, was still very much a city of immigrants. The old-guard Yankees were there, to be sure, but immigrants—especially from northern Europe—were a vital force in the growing city. Swedish, Norwegian, German, Irish and other accents could be heard on the streets and many Swedish and Norwegian Lutheran churches still held Sunday services in the languages of the "old countries."

Some of the newcomers became American success stories, hailed and sometimes envied by their fellow immigrants because of their rise in life. One of these was Swan J. Turnblad, a poor boy from one of Sweden's poorest provinces, who made it big with a Swedish-language newspaper, nearly went bankrupt, recovered and eventually left a legacy that is still a cherished part of Swedish-American life. This is the story of Turnblad and the house he built, which is now the American Swedish Institute at 2600 Park Avenue.

Several months after his wife Christina died in September of 1929, Turnblad and his quiet daughter Lillian moved into a fifth-floor apartment in the southwest corner of the brand-new building at 2615 Park Avenue near downtown Minneapolis. Turnblad often gazed out the window at his former home—the imposing residence at 2600 Park Avenue that many Minnesota residents now call "the castle"—watching the people go in and out of the house.

Turnblad, who had made what some people called a fortune with his Swedish-language newspaper, *Svenska Amerikanska Posten,* had turned his magnificent house over to the newly established American Institute of Swedish Arts, Literature and Science in 1929 to be used as a cultural center, but he still took a proprietary interest in it. According to Pearl Lundeberg Tolzman, daughter of Turnblad's friend, the Rev. Axel Lundeberg, "After the donation of the mansion, Turnblad did not appear too often there but remained in his apartment across the street and remarked to my father that he watched the people come and go and hoped that his beautiful oriental rugs would not be soiled!"[1]

What was he like—this Swedish immigrant with a genius for making money and the house-proud soul of a Småland farmer? Even now, decades after his death, visitors to his magnificent house are curious about the man who built it. There is no easy way to describe him, for Turnblad, like most people, was a bundle of contradictions. He could be at various times kind and sentimental or stern

Swan J. Turnblad, publisher of the Svenska Amerikanska Posten *and later founder of the American Swedish Institute, as a young man.*

Swan J. Turnblad, utgivare av Svenska Amerikanska Posten och senare grundare av American Swedish Institute, som ung.

A 1903 issue of the **Svenska Amerikanska Posten** *commemorated the convention of the American Union of Swedish Singers.*

Ett nummer av **Svenska Amerikanska Posten, från år 1903, till minne av American Union of Swedish Singers kongress.**

Olof Månsson and his family, including the son later known as Swan J. Turnblad, lived in this house in the community of Långhult in Småland, Sweden, before emigrating to the United States.

Olof Månsson och hans familj, med den son som senare fick namnet Swan J. Turnblad, bodde i detta hus i Långhult i Småland innan de emigrerade till USA.

and demanding. He was on occasion very generous and sometimes a penny-pincher. Some of his contemporaries said he and his family kept to themselves, but records of social and civic events he was involved in suggest otherwise.

Notes: [1]Memoir of Pearl Lundeberg Tolzman in the American Swedish Institute's archives, July, 1989.

Swan Turnblad's Life in Sweden

The facts of Swan J. Turnblad's life are easy to ascertain. He and his family were among the 1.25 million Swedes who immigrated to the United States in the 19th and early 20th centuries. Turnblad was born on Oct. 7, 1860 in Tubbamåla,[2] the land his parents farmed in Vislanda parish in the county of Kronoberg, in the province of Småland in southern Sweden. His parents, Ingjerd Månsdotter and Olof Månsson, had him christened Sven Johan on the day of his birth.[3] At that time, children in Sweden traditionally formed their last names from the possessive form of their father's first name, followed by "son" or "dotter." Rightly, then, Sven Johan should have been called Olofsson. When the family emigrated to the United States, the family, like many Scandinavian immigrants, used another name, Turnblad. Consequently, the boy who began life in Sweden as Sven Johan Olofsson later Americanized his first name to "Swan," and was known as Swan J. Turnblad for the rest of his years.

A map of Tubbamåla shows that four of the five farms in the tiny hamlet are long and narrow, with the houses and outbuildings of several of them clustered together on the north end of Tubbamåla, close to the road. The little community was south of the present town of Vislanda, not terribly far north of the Blekinge provincial boundary.[4]

Olof Månsson was trying to raise a big family on one of these small farms. Sven Johan was the youngest of Månsson's eleven children from two marriages. There was a great span in the ages of the children. One of Sven Johan's half-brothers, Peter Olofsson, was born in 1839, making him 21 years old when Sven Johan was born. Peter Olofsson left for America in 1864 and settled in Vasa, Minnesota, where his father and family, including Sven Johan, later joined him.

It was several more years before the Månssons decided to emigrate. Meanwhile, when Sven Johan was six years old, they had moved from the Tubbamåla farm first to Långhult, Södregård (south farm) and later to Norregård (north farm), in the parish of Ryssby but still in Kronoberg County. Although the exact reasons for deciding to emigrate are not explicitly stated in print, it was most likely a combination of bad weather and crop failures that spurred them to leave Sweden.

Even under favorable circumstances, Småland, a beautiful but stone-filled place where farmers seemed to raise more rocks than grain, was a difficult area to farm. Certainly the sequence of events in the late 1860s was the last straw for many emigrants, who were already hearing of America as the new promised land. The cold winter of 1867 in Sweden was followed by an unseasonably cold summer and fall and most farmers couldn't harvest enough seed corn to plant the following spring. The hot, dry summer of 1868 also meant a crop failure. People began to starve and ate anything that could be eaten, including grinding up the inner membrane of birch trees into a "flour" from which a sort of bread could be made. This "bark-bread" is described in Wilhelm Moberg's *A History of the Swedish People: From Renaissance to Revolution,* published by Pantheon Books in 1973.

It is not known if the Månssons suffered from the famine, but it was the cause of much of the emigration during those years. Although almost 135,000 Swedes immigrated to the United States in a 14-year period from 1863 to 1877, 40 percent of that total left in 1868 and 1869. In all, from 1845 until 1930, when emigration from Sweden had slowed to a trickle, approximately 1,250,000 Swedes—between 20 and 25 percent of the population—had left their homeland for North America. Only Ireland, Norway and Iceland had a greater percentage of emigrants.[5]

Notes: [2]Tubbemåla is the modern spelling. [3]This and much of the material to follow is from extensive research done by Lawrence Hammerstrom, an ASI member, on Swan J. Turnblad, his family and the American Swedish Institute. [4]An 1856 map of Tubbamåla is in the office of the director of the American Swedish Institute in Minneapolis, Minnesota. [5]John Rice "The Swedes," in *They Chose Minnesota—A Survey of the State's Ethnic Groups,* edited by June Drenning Holmquist (Minnesota Historical Society Press, 1981) p. 254.

An 1856 map of Tubbamåla, Sweden, shows the farm where Swan J. Turnblad was born.

En karta över Tubbamåla från 1856 visar bondgården där Swan J. Turnblad föddes.

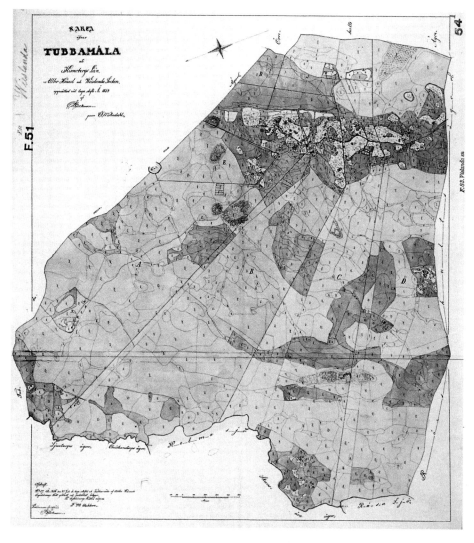

Courtesy of the Minnesota Historical Society

The Lure of America

This map of Minnesota appeared in an 1887 atlas.

Denna karta över Minnesota fanns i en kartbok från 1887.

Just as famine pushed Swedes out of their country, the offer of free land pulled them toward the United States. In 1862, the U.S. Congress passed the Homestead Act, which gave 160 acres to U.S. citizens of legal age and also those who had declared that they wanted to become citizens. If the homesteaders worked the land and built some sort of structure on the land and remained there for five years, the land was theirs, free and clear. Another factor luring Swedes to the United States was the appearance of the so-called America letters. Written by Swedish immigrants, they were printed in local papers, usually extolling the wonders of the United States.

The state of Minnesota conducted its own campaign to lure emigrants from Scandinavia. The Minnesota Board of Immigration published a brochure in Swedish with the long title: *Minnesota and its advantages for the immigrant, containing a description of the state's history, geography, government, cities, rivers, lakes, forests, climate, soil, minerals, railroads, commerce, industries, etc., which are of interest and importance for those seeking their homes in the West.*[6]

In Minnesota, there was plenty of land available for homesteading. In 1851, two treaties made by the federal government with the Dakota Indians meant that much of southern Minnesota was now in the hands of the United States. The Dakota, many of whom agreed to the treaties because they felt forced to do so, were relegated first to two reservations and later one small reservation along the Minnesota River. These treaties and their ramifications were instrumental in causing the U.S.-Dakota Conflict of 1862, which resulted in the deaths of nearly 500 settlers and an unknown number of Dakota. These events were still fresh in the minds of Minnesotans in the late 1860s when the great mass of immigrants began arriving from Sweden.

Notes: [6]Chicago, 1867. Hans Mattson was the author.

S.S. CITY OF NEW YORK No 2.   INMAN.

The Månsson/Turnblad family arrived in New York City aboard the S.S. City of New York.

Familjen Månsson/Turnblad anlände till New York City ombord på S.S. City of New York.

Courtesy of the Peabody Essex Museum, Salem, Massachusetts.

The Voyage to America

Whatever their personal reasons for deciding to leave their farm and their country, Olof Månsson and his family, including the nearly eight-year-old Sven Johan, left Sweden in 1868 and—like many emigrants—went first to Liverpool, England, where they boarded the *S.S. City of New York,* arriving in New York City on Sept. 25, 1868. The Månsson-Turnblads sailed steerage.[7] On the same ship, but in the more expensive cabin class, was Ole Bull, the noted Norwegian violinist and founder of the short-lived Utopian community of Oleanna in Pennsylvania in 1852.[8]

The Turnblads followed a well-worn path across the ocean. Most of the Swedish immigrants went from Göteborg, Sweden, by small ships to Hull, England, and then by train to Liverpool, where they boarded larger ships for the trans-Atlantic voyage.[9] The long Atlantic crossing was shortened considerably in the 1860s when steamships instead of sailing ships became common and ticket prices became cheaper. One-way passage between Göteborg and Chicago, Illinois, cost about $41.[10] The record for the England-New York

Swedish explanations were printed on this map of the docks area in Liverpool, England.

På denna karta över hamnen i Liverpool, England, fanns förklaringar på svenska.

13

City of Baltimore made good headway. The food was good and the treatment by officers and crew, all one could desire.

"Occupation aboard varied greatly. Many read and sang songs while others danced to the music of an accordion; others engaged in fingerpulling and wrestling and many other pastimes were devised, more than I can name. The weather was beautiful the whole time we were in the Atlantic and the days were all alike.

"On the morning of June 29 the lookout shouted 'land'...Shortly before sunset, Saturday, June 29, the *City of Baltimore* cast anchor and we had arrived in the highly publicized Land in the West. The voyage over the Atlantic from Liverpool to New York was made in nine days and six hours, the fastest crossing up to that date."[12]

Notes: [7]Family history by Dr. Paul R. Fridlund, Turnblad's great-nephew, in the archives of the American Swedish Institute. [8]*Dictionary of American History Vol. V,* (New York: Charles Scribner's Sons, 1976) p. 152. [9]*From Sweden to America,* (Minneapolis: University of Minnesota Press, 1976), p. 189. [10]Lars Ljungmark, *Swedish Exodus.* Translated by Kermit Westerberg. (Carbondale and Edwardsville Illinois: Southern Illinois University Press for Swedish Pioneer Historical Society, 1979) p. 44. [11]Arnold H. Barton, *Letters from the Promised Land: Swedes in America: 1840-1914.* (Minneapolis: University of Minnesota Press, 1975), p. 123. [12]Ibid.

Passengers aboard immigrant ships passed the long journey on deck in good weather, as this image from a stereo card shows.

Passagerare ombord på immi-grantfartyg tillbringade den långa resan uppe på däck då vädret tillät, vilket vi kan se på detta stereografiska kort.

trip in the early steamship days was nine days and six hours in 1867 aboard the *City of Baltimore* between Liverpool and New York, the same route the Turnblads took a year later.[11]

A passenger on the *City of Baltimore* left a detailed account of his trip in the collection of immigrant letters, *Letters from the Promised Land: Swedes in America: 1840-1914.* The passenger, Johannes Swenson, wrote enthusiastically about his trip 50 years after, in 1917:

"...The weather was beautiful. The sea was calm and the

Little Town on the Prairie

Before Ellis Island facilities opened later in the 19th century, all new immigrants debarked on the east side of Manhattan, at a processing place called Castle Garden. After they arrived in the United States and were done with the formalities of entering the country at Castle Garden, the Turnblads probably traveled onwards to Minnesota by train, from New York to Chicago and thence to Red Wing, Minnesota, a few miles from their destination in Vasa. The town of Vasa, which still exists as a small community in southeastern Minnesota, not far inland from the Mississippi River, is on open prairie land. One early resident was Eric Norelius, a Lutheran pastor and one of the leading figures in the Augustana Lutheran Synod. Names on the plats of land in 1877 are resoundingly Scandinavian: Anderson, Olson, Johnson, Ljungren, Swanson, Peterson, etc. Even the names that don't sound Scandinavian, Turner, for example, are often Americanized names for Swedish or Norwegian immigrants.[13]

Earlier, Hans Mattson—another Swedish immigrant who later became Minnesota's Secretary of State—founded the little settlement. Coincidentally, all three Vasa residents—Swan Turnblad, Norelius and Mattson—were to be associated with two of the leading Swedish language newspapers in Minnesota: Turnblad with the *Svenska Amerikanska Posten*,

Courtesy of the Vasa Lutheran Church

Mattson and Norelius and his descendants with the *Minnesota Stats Tidning*.[14]

Little is known about Turnblad's life on the farm and growing up in Vasa. Records show he was confirmed at Vasa's Swedish Lutheran Church in May of 1876. It is believed that he printed an arithmetic book for his teacher, P.T. Lindholm, in 1877. If he did, it was the first evidence of his skill in setting type by hand, a profession he later pursued when he moved to Minneapolis in 1879.[15]

An 1875 census of Vasa shows what is probably

A sketch of the Turnblad farmstead from Vasa Illustrata, an account of the early days of Vasa Lutheran Church in Vasa, Minnesota, published in 1905.

En skiss av familjen Turnblads bondgård från Vasa Illustrata, en redogörelse för den första tiden i Vasa, Minnesota, publicerad 1905.

An early photo of Swan J. Turnblad, believed to be his confirmation photograph, shows him with a very determined look.

Swan J. Turnblad ser mycket bestämd ut på detta foto, troligtvis från hans konfirmation.

Swan Turnblad's family, although the spellings varied from earlier spellings. His father was listed as Ola Turnblad, age 63; his mother as Inga, age 57. His brother Magnus was then 17 and Sven Johan himself, under that name, was 14 years old.[16]

Notes: [13]1877 plat from the Goodhue County Historical Society archives. [14]Nyberg, Janet, "Swedish Language Newspapers in Minnesota," in *Perspectives on Swedish Immigration*, edited by Nils Hasselmo, Swedish Pioneer Historical Society and University of Minnesota Duluth (Chicago and Duluth, 1978), p. 244-255. [15]Lawrence G. Hammerstrom, *A Chronology of the Events in the Lives of Swan Johan Turnblad, Christina Nilsson Turnblad, Lillian Zenobia Turnblad*, December, 1997. [16]*Vasa Census*, 1875, from the Goodhue County Historical Society archives.

Swan J. and Christina Turnblad were married in Augustana Lutheran Church (above) in Minneapolis in 1883.

Swan J. och Christina Turnblad gifte sig i Augustana Lutheran Church (ovan) i Minneapolis år 1883.

Swan and Christina Turnblad

The first evidence of Swan Turnblad in Minneapolis came in 1880, when the U.S. Census showed him as a compositor living as a boarder at 127 Cedar Avenue in Minneapolis with his sister and brother-in-law, Mary and Charles Fridlund. The *Minneapolis City Directory* of 1881-1883 lists Turnblad at the same address, working as a compositor for the *Minnesota Stats Tidning.*[17]

It was around the same time that Turnblad's future wife, Christina Nilsson, moved to Minneapolis. Christina, whose name was originally Kerstin, was born and baptized on Feb. 25, 1861, at Tångeråsen, in Offerdal parish in Jämtland County, Sweden. Her parents were Gabriel Nilsson and Brita Göransdotter. Her last name has been spelled in various ways: Nilsson, Nilson and Nelson. When she was 14, in 1875, her father and her brother, Göran, emigrated to the United States and each of them homesteaded near Slayton, in Murray County in southern Minnesota. Christina and her brother, Simon, followed them in 1876, via Trondheim, Norway, and their mother and a sister, also named Brita, followed in turn in May of 1877. Augustana

Lutheran Church records show that Christina was confirmed in a Murray County church in 1878.

In the February she turned 18, in 1879, Christina began working as a "dining room girl" for Worthington, Minnesota, hotelkeeper Daniel Shell. She worked there for one year and received $153.53 for the entire year.[18]

Christina's family was unlucky in the New World. Her brother Göran died from tuberculosis in 1879 and her mother succumbed to the same disease in 1881. Christina probably moved to Minneapolis in the early 1880s, as she is listed in the 1882-1883 *Minneapolis City Directory* as a clerk in Carlson's Book Store, living at 1204 South 2nd Street in Minneapolis. She and Turnblad met at a temperance meeting or dance and were married on April 28, 1883, in Augustana Lutheran Church in Minneapolis, slightly more than two months before her father died of a hernia. Her sister, Brita, moved to Minneapolis to be with the young married Turnblads.

But tuberculosis wasn't done with Christina's family: her brother Simon Nilsson died of the disease in May of 1884, leaving a wife and month-old daughter, Anna Severine. Brita Nilsson, Christina's sister died, also of tuberculosis the following year. Swan Turnblad was appointed guardian of Anna Severine, Christina Turnblad's niece.

The bright spot amid all this tragedy was the birth of the Turnblads' only child, Lillian Zenobia, who was born on Sept. 2, 1884. She was baptized several weeks later at Augustana Lutheran Church. Artistic

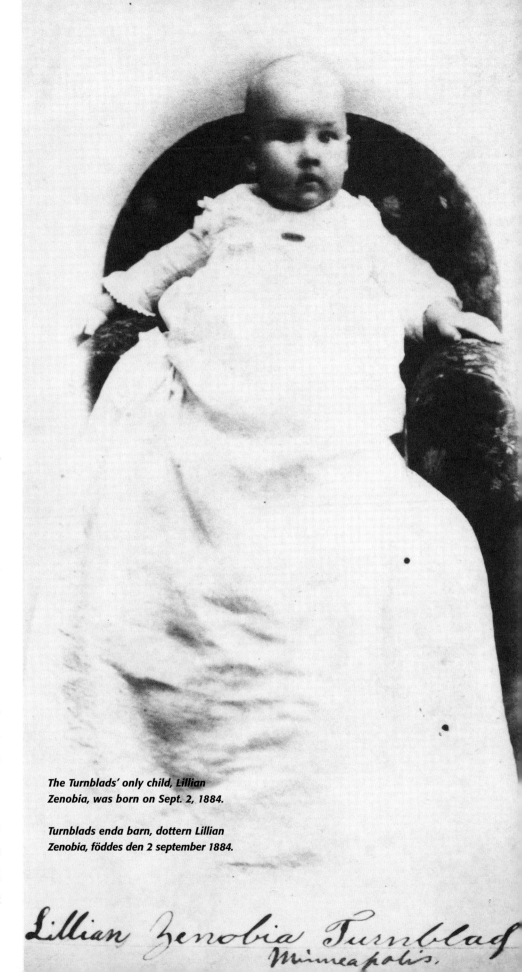

The Turnblads' only child, Lillian Zenobia, was born on Sept. 2, 1884.

Turnblads enda barn, dottern Lillian Zenobia, föddes den 2 september 1884.

Lillian Zenobia Turnblad Minneapolis.

Swan J. Turnblad remained active in fraternal organizations and civic affairs until late in life.

Swan J. Turnblad var aktiv i broderskapsorganisationer och kommunala sammanhang även på äldre dagar.

When Turnblad was elevated to a 32nd degree Mason in 1899, he received this elaborate certificate.

När Turnblad blev frimurare av 32:a graden år 1899 fick han detta eleganta diplom.

and musical, Lillian was educated at the Northwestern Conservatory of Music and later at St. Joseph's Academy in St. Paul. She finished her education at the Convent of the Sacred Heart in Montréal, Canada. Upon her graduation, she was awarded a medal and a blue ribbon. All graduates got medals, but the blue ribbon was a special award given for initiative and good conduct.

Notes: [17]Hammerstrom. [18]Ibid.

The Turnblads were a family of three—Swan J., his wife Christina and their daughter Lillian—in this photo taken around 1890.

Tre i familjen-Swan J., hustrun Christina och dottern Lillian-på detta foto taget omkring år 1890.

Turnblad as a Public Figure

Over the years, Swan Turnblad joined many fraternal and other organizations and was active in civic affairs. Some of his and also Christina Turnblad's activities revolved around the temperance movement. They were members of the Freya Society, which advocated temperance; Swan Turnblad was elected treasurer of the Society in 1885. The temperance meetings weren't totally without fun, however. An 1889 newspaper account tells of the Turnblads being "unceremoniously" visited and feted on a Saturday night by about 30 members of the Freya Society, who sang, gave recitations, read poetry and made speeches, "which were responded to heartily by the host." The Turnblads were presented with an engraved silver water pitcher and stand.[19]

Turnblad apparently had a wry sense of humor, as shown in the dinner menu for the dinner the Turnblads gave "in honor of the newspaperman and author" Dr. V. Hugo Wickström in May of 1901. The cover of the menu reproduced a page from the *JämtlandsPosten,* which Wickström edited. Inside, the menu included "Press-Soppa" [press soup], "Journalist-Frikadeller," [journalist meat patties], "Rapportör-Frukt (Icke förbjuden)" [reporter's fruit—(not forbidden)] and "Tryckfrihets-Oliver" [freedom of the press olives].[20]

In 1898, Turnblad joined the Minnesota Blue Lodge #224, a Masonic organization. He continued up through the ranks of Masonry, achieving the highest level—the 33rd degree in the Scottish Rite. As a Mason, he was eligible to join the Shriners, which he did in 1899; he became a life member. In 1901, he also joined the Benevolent and Protective Order of the Elks.

In his Shriner days, he may have often visited the Zuhrah Shrine headquarters, just across 26th Street from his own house at 2600 Park Avenue. The building housing the Shrine was started at the turn of the century and completed, except for the marvelous carving and ornamentation done by Norwegian and Swedish artisans, in 1902. It was built and owned by Charles Harrington. The Shriners bought the house in 1928, after Harrington's death. It now contains a beautiful brass and ruby glass lamp that was once in the Turnblad house.

A frequent committee member, Turnblad was on the 1888 committee to celebrate the 250th

Turnblad's sense of humor shows in the menu for a dinner honoring the editor of Jämtlands-Posten, *a leading Swedish newspaper.*

Man kan här se att Turnblad hade humor. Hedersgäst var redaktören på regionaltidningen JämtlandsPosten.

Turnblad seems to be peeking around the pillar in the right background at the Odin Club's Washington's birthday party. He was a charter member of the club.

Turnblad verkar kika fram bakom en pelare till höger på Odin Club där man firade Washingtons födelsedag. Han var en av de ursprungliga medlemmarna i klubben.

Turnblad was proud of being the first man in Minneapolis to own a commercially produced automobile. He decked his second car out with flowers for a parade in 1903.

Turnblad var stolt över att vara den förste som ägde en kommersiellt tillverkad bil i Minneapolis. Han prydde sin andra bil med blommor för en parad 1903.

Turnblad was a supporter of William Jennings Bryan, who was nominated as the Democratic candidate for president in 1896, 1900 and 1908 and lost each time. Bryan is second from right in the front row. Turnblad is at left in back row.

Turnblad stödde William Jennings Bryan som nominerades till det demokratiska partiets presidentkandidat 1896, 1900 och 1908 och förlorade varje gång.

anniversary of the first Swedish colony in the United States. In 1893, he was on the committee to discuss whether to build a Swedish hospital in Minneapolis and he later served on a committee that served as the hospital board until its first annual meeting could be held. He sat on the committee for the John Ericsson Memorial Association in 1897 and years later, when a statue of the Swedish mechanical genius was unveiled in Washington, D.C. in 1926, Turnblad was listed as the 3rd Vice Chairman of the Ericsson Memorial Committee.

He was appointed to the Board of Managers for the Minnesota State Reformatory in 1899 by Governor John Lind, with the term ending in 1905 and was for a time on the General Staff of the Minnesota National Guard. He had the title of "Colonel and Aide-de-Camp" until his term expired in 1915. He was also on the board of the Swedish-American Bank and was appointed to the State Board of Visitors for Public Institutions for a term starting in 1917 and ending in 1923.[21]

Turnblad may also have remembered what it was like to be hungry in Sweden when he led a campaign that raised $20,000 for the relief of starving people in the north of Sweden in 1902 when crops failed, as they did just before Turnblad left Sweden for America many years before. More than two decades later, in 1926, Turnblad was presented with the Order of the North Star by Swedish Vice-Consul Nils L. Jaenson on behalf of the King of Sweden for his fund-raising work during the famine.[22] The order is now in the collection of the American Swedish Institute.

He never ran for public office, though he became an American citizen in 1895 and therefore could have sought elective office. He was active in politics, however. Although he was listed as the secretary of the North Star Republican Club on Dec. 8, 1896, Turnblad was later a member of the Democratic party.

He was a delegate to Democratic national conventions, in 1904 and 1908. For the 1900 convention, in Omaha, Nebraska, Turnblad sent the Posten Brass Band, which he financed, to lead a parade put on for William Jennings Bryan,[23]

who was nominated for president that year and also in 1896 and 1908—he lost all three times to the Republican nominee.

Notes: [19]*Minneapolis Times,* Feb. 26, 1889. [20]Menu for 1901 Wickström dinner, ASI archives. [21]Information on Turnblad's civic activities from the Hammerstrom chronology and the ASI archives. [22]*Minneapolis Tribune,* Oct. 7, 1930. [23]Emil Berglund, "An Intimate Account of the Founding" in *American Swedish Institute Bulletin,* (1960:XV), p. 7.

Swan J. Turnblad, shown here in uniform, was a colonel and aide-de-camp on the general staff of the Minnesota National Guard, a term that ended in 1915.

Swan J. Turnblad, här i uniform, var överste och adjutant vid staben i Minnesotas hemvärn, ett uppdrag som avslutades år 1915.

The Private Life and Travels of Swan J. Turnblad

Swan Turnblad was apparently not the remote figure some people imagined him to be. Certainly Linnea Osman Swanson, who worked with Turnblad after he turned the house over to the Swedish-American community, said otherwise. Swanson, interviewed by *Minneapolis Star* columnist Barbara Flanagan in a column published on Dec. 9, 1969, had this to say about Turnblad:

"Mr. Turnblad looked like a good Swedish farmer. He had a good strong Swedish face with light brown hair and bright blue eyes. He was the type of man who commanded respect. Stern-looking, but he had a good sense of humor. He just had to have certain people around him before he'd crack

a smile...Once in a while he'd share my lunch and we'd always make plenty of coffee. Oh, he was a coffee-drinker.

"He'd tell me how tickled he was that people could be so nice and want to help make the museum a beautiful place to visit."[24]

The Turnblads were great travelers and Swan Turnblad often sent reports describing his travels, which were printed in weekly installments in the *Svenska Amerikanska Posten.* The reports were accompanied by photos in the later reports; it is most likely that the photos were from the newspaper's files. Turnblad signed each "letter"

The Svenska Amerikanska Posten sponsored a brass band, which played for the Democratic National Convention in Omaha in 1900.

Svenska Amerikanska Posten bekostade en mässingsorkester som spelade vid det demokratiska partiets nationella konvent i Omaha år 1900.

to readers in his flowing script and usually included good wishes to them or another friendly closing statement.

While no one knows if Turnblad's reports were edited by the *Posten* staff before they were printed, the subject matter shows that Turnblad was an astute observer, who mixed details with his own opinions in describing events of the day and places he went. He had very firm opinions and was not afraid to see them in print. He could also be quite sentimental, especially when he was writing about Sweden. Although his wife and daughter went along with him, he almost never mentions them. One of few references to Christina Turnblad, in his report on a 1902 journey, notes in passing that she was an early riser.

The Turnblads' first trip abroad was to Sweden and Norway in June of 1895. Two summers later, the family sailed to Europe, visiting England, France, Belgium, Germany, Denmark and Sweden. Turnblad and his family were seen off in style at the Milwaukee Depot in downtown Minneapolis on May 12.

Not only friends, acquaintances and family members were among the crowd to wave good-bye, but C.H. Bothman, whose company had made most of Turnblad's travel arrangements, and his assistant were there to supervise the loading of the baggage. Ever the astute businessman (Bothman also was an advertiser in the *Posten*), Turnblad put in a brief plug for the Bothman business, including the address.[25]

One of the early stops on the tour was Paris. And, like so many visitors to Paris through the years, Turnblad had difficulty communicating with the French. He wrote, "It is comical to go out, because only in the largest hotels do you find English-speaking service people. Therefore, you have to make use of sign language in most cases."[26]

Turnblad wrote joyfully of his return to Sweden, via Malmö: "It seems so homelike and pleasant... to hear pure Swedish from Svea's sons and daughters, such as we haven't heard since we left Minneapolis."[27] On June 7, Turnblad returned to his birthplace in Vislanda Parish in southern Sweden. He was quite obviously deeply affected, writing, in the July 6, 1897, edition of the *Posten,* under a headline that said, "Dear Old Memories:"

> "Yesterday was a day that I will long keep in my memory. I had the pleasure of visiting the place and the cottage where my cradle stood, namely Norregård (north farm) in Tubbamåla."

At Tubbamåla, the current occupant of the house, Petter August Magnusson, whose father had purchased it from Turnblad's father, invited the Turnblads in for coffee and rolls. Turnblad noted he was only six years old when the family moved from Tubbamåla, and wrote that the only thing he remembered from that time was a big rock near the door of the cottage. He wrote, a touch ruefully it seems, that the rock had been removed because it spoiled the view from the cottage window. The fruit trees that his father had planted almost 25 years previously, he added, were still there and still bearing fruit.

Turnblad's nostalgia tour to Tubbamåla also took him to another house, on the Södregård (south farm) where Samuel Magnusson had known the whole Turnblad clan. They were invited in for coffee and waffles and Turnblad had a surprise: "Here, remarkably enough, I met his sister, Elin Magnusson, who was my godmother." Tears were in her eyes, he noted, when she talked about old memories and inquired about her old playmate, Turnblad's aunt, who had emigrated to America.

Turnblad describes the stony Småland landscape, as seen on the trip and writes, "I wasn't surprised that so many Smålanders go to America and that they could rise up, like John Lind (editor's note: Lind was a Minnesota governor)...because it is certain that it is their inheritance of their homeland's firm character and initiative and not some family fortune that was the reason for them to rise in the world.

He ended by saying, "I have probably now been going on too much about so-called private things, but 'deraf hjertat fullt är, deraf taler munnen,' ("It is from the fullness of the heart that the mouth speaks," Matthew 34:12), and I hope therefore to be forgiven."[28]

On the same trip to Sweden, Turnblad stopped in Göteborg, Sweden, where he bought the library of J. B. Gans—6,000 volumes—which he later let subscribers to the *Svenska Amerikanska Posten* borrow. Some of the books are now displayed in the ASI archives or in the mansion's library.

In 1899, the Turnblads visited Europe again—this

time Belgium, the Netherlands, Germany, Denmark, Sweden, Switzerland, Italy and France. In France, according to an account published by the *Minneapolis Journal,* Turnblad attended some of the trial surrounding the notorious Dreyfus incident. Alfred Dreyfus, a French Army officer, had earlier been convicted—unjustly—of treason and his case was being retried.

In April of 1902, the Turnblads left on a sojourn to Italy, Greece, Turkey, Russia, Finland and Sweden.

The Turnblads sat for this photo on a trip to Sweden. Swan Turnblad is at right; next to him are Christina (standing) and Lillian (seated). The others are not identified.

Turnblads poserade för detta foto under ett besök i Sverige. Swan Turnblad till höger; bred-vid honom Christina (stående) och Lillian (sittande). Övriga ej identifierade.

Among the tourists sailing were ten Italians who had been deported by the U.S. government because of their poverty, according to Turnblad. He wrote with great compassion about their situation, perhaps remembering his own early days:

> "They had dreamt about America as a promised land, had managed to scrape together enough means for the trip but were not allowed to stay...Well, it is quite right that the American government not allow such to remain here but it is hard to see these poor people be so disappointed in their expectations and forced to return to their old surroundings and meager accommodations, losing their trip fare that perhaps with pain and privation they had saved up for a long time. Their hope of a brighter future was forever completely vanished. Poor people, their lot is hard."[29]

On the same voyage, Mrs. Turnblad, whom Turnblad describes as an early riser, was on deck and witnessed the suicide of a man who had been an acrobat on tour in the United States. Lifeboats were launched to recover the man, but they failed to find him. A collection was taken up for the man's young son, Turnblad wrote.

The Turnblads' first stop on the 1902 journey was Gibraltar, where they saw the fortress. Then they went on to Italy, where they visited the house where Christopher Columbus was born, the Leaning Tower of Pisa, Mt. Vesuvius, Pompeii and the Blue Grotto on the Isle of Capri. In Rome, the Turnblads, along with 75 Dutch tourists, had a so-called "private" audience with Pope Leo XIII. They continued on their way, visiting the Parthenon and the Acropolis in Greece and the Kremlin in Moscow before journeying from Constantinople to Odessa in Russia over the Black Sea. The trip concluded with visits to Finland, Sweden and Denmark before the Turnblads headed home.

He enjoyed his brief stay in Greece, writing:

> "I had expected to find the Greeks just as unpleasant as the Italians. After over three weeks' visit among the emotional Italians, who on every occasion seek to fleece the tourists, it seems rather pleasant to come among people who are unusually well behaved, courteous and orderly (at least those we came into contact with here in Athens) and are very much like the Swedes. In all the lands I have visited I have never seen such people that are so like the Swedes as the Greeks."[30]

Could Turnblad have been spied upon during this trip? He thought so, writing from Russia:

> "I can relate to you an example of something very amusing, we were spied upon by a Turkish or Russian spy during the whole way from Naples to Athens and from there to Constantinople and to Odessa. That person was a pale-faced woman. I had noticed her on board the ship after we left Naples. She pretended not to understand English, only French and Russian but several times when we ate, I noticed that she understood everything that was said. When we came on board at Athens, again she was at our table, also when we came to our table on the Russian ship. I expect that we will see her again before we leave Russia."[31]

Notes: [24]*Minneapolis Star,* Dec. 9, 1969. p. 1C. [25]*SAP,* June 1, 1897. [26]Ibid., June 15, 1897. [27]Ibid., July 6, 1897. [28]Ibid. [29]Ibid., May 13, 1902. [30]Ibid., June 24, 1902. [31]Ibid., July 15, 1902.

A Thoroughly Modern Man

Swan Turnblad was thoroughly modern in his outlook and habits. He bought the latest machinery for his newspaper and he was equally forward-looking for himself. He was the first person in Minneapolis to own an automobile. It was a Waverley Electric made in Indianapolis, Indiana, in 1899. It cost Turnblad $1,250, not including the freight charges.

According to Robert R. Johnson, a member of the American Swedish Institute who has done a great deal of research on Swan Turnblad's cars, Turnblad's Waverley was the first commercially manufactured automobile in Minneapolis. It arrived in town in March, 1900. Automobiles were called "horseless carriages" at that time and the open Waverley resembled exactly that—a carriage with a steering tiller instead of a team of horses. It caused much comment. An article in the *Minneapolis Journal* of April 10, 1900, said:

"The first private electric automobile appeared on the streets last evening. It belongs to Swan J. Turnblad, proprietor of the *Svenska Amerikanska Posten,* and created somewhat of a sensation as it rolled along Nicollet Avenue carrying the owner and a party of friends. The vehicle is one of the latest patterns with all the latest improvements. It will run from thirty to forty miles without being recharged and it can be regulated to five different degrees of speed. Mr. Turnblad has placed a

Below is a letter to the editor of the *Minneapolis Journal* of July 25, 1900, in which Turnblad responds to an earlier article about the unreliability of automobiles.

To the editor of the *Journal:*

In your Saturday issue I noticed an article headed "They Get Habits On" in regard to automobiles, saying that breakdowns of autos have occurred so often that the confidence of auto owners is shaken, etc.

I believe I was the first owner of an auto (electric) in this city having had one of the Waverly (editor's note: Waverley was the correct spelling) Dos-a-Dos since early last spring. So far I have never had a hitch or breakdown having used my vehicle more or less every day and evening since I got it, running from five to thirty-five miles each trip, making all hills and grades in the vicinity of Minneapolis with four of us in it, and I believe you do an injustice and misrepresent the autos in your article.

A breakdown may and will happen to any vehicle sometimes but I feel just as safe of return home in my electric auto as I would after a pair of lively horses.

The electric auto has several advantages over a rig drawn by horses. First, it is always ready; secondly, it never gets tired out, that is, until the charge is consumed and with my auto I can travel on a level roadbed sixty miles, but on ups and downs, as we have them here around Minneapolis, probably only fifty miles without recharging. The third reason why I value my auto ahead of a rig drawn by horses is the fact that it is clean and breezy, kicking up no dirt or dust, giving the full benefits of the bracing air, especially so in hot weather, when horses will sweat and when dusty or muddy, they will kick up the dust and dirt.

I have no experience with steam or gasoline autos but believe that if they are properly understood and taken care of they will prove satisfactory, but I am sure that any electric rig, if they act and serve as well as mine has done so far, will be placed ahead of a horse rig. I would not trade my electric auto, providing I could not buy another one, for any span of horses and Victoria in Minneapolis even if it included a coachman's services free of charge for one year, and would not sell my electric auto at any price if I could not buy another one.

I have heard the remark it is not enough of a sport to ride in an auto. Well, try <u>once</u> going at a speed of twenty-two or twenty-three miles an hour and I believe such parties will find it sport enough. I can get home from Lake Harriet to 1511 Stevens Avenue in less than fifteen minutes and without my auto-horse sweaty or tired out, run the rig into the barn, put the charging plug into same and in a few minutes it is again ready for fifty or sixty miles run.

Another reason why I prefer an auto instead of a horse rig is that it is less expensive, costing only about one-half cents per running mile, and it does not eat oats when not used. I have so far not spent a dollar on repairs or wear and tear, used very little oil and grease as everything is fitted with ball bearings.

I am no agent for any company, and the above is written wholly to protest against the injustice done the autos as a whole and mine in particular, in that your article above referred to does not make any exceptions.

—-Swan J. Turnblad

Swan J. Turnblad takes the tiller of his Waverley Electric, the first commercially produced automobile owned by a Minneapolis resident.

Swan J. Turnblad vid ratten i sin Waverley Electric, den första kommersiellt tillverkade bil som ägdes av en Minneapolisbo.

small electric plant in his barn with which he recharges the carriage whenever necessary."[32]

Because he was the first in the city to own a car, Turnblad was chosen to lead a procession of 13 automobiles that set out from the courthouse in downtown Minneapolis on a journey from Minneapolis to Wayzata on Aug. 10, 1900. Eight of the vehicles reached their goal, the Lafayette Club on the shore of Lake Minnetonka. The fastest car made the 12-mile trip in 42 minutes—faster than today's cars can cover the same distance if traffic is heavy. Turnblad's Waverley electric, more limited than cars with gasoline engines, and four other cars didn't make it that far, however. Turnblad and his wife also showed up in the Waverley taking a turn around the track normally used for horse races during the Minnesota State Fair in September of 1900. The Waverley was one of about 40 'horseless carriages' in the parade.

Turnblad's second car was a 1903 Knox Waterless, an air-cooled vehicle with one cylinder. It held two passengers and there was a fold-out seat in front for two more. Next Turnblad bought a 1908 Winton Touring car. It had six cylinders and was rated at 48 horsepower. It cost $4,500 and had licenses for both the state and the city of Minneapolis. The 1910 state license was number 2600, the same as Turnblad's magnificent new house at 2600 Park Avenue. Was this mere coincidence or did Turnblad have one of the first vanity plates? His fourth automobile was a 1910 enclosed Columbus Electric, which held four passengers. The 1911 and 1912 Minnesota license plates

were registered in Christina Turnblad's name.

His last two cars were a Premier, reportedly manufactured in 1918, about which little is known, and a 1926 Chandler sedan. The Chandler was said to have been purchased at a Minneapolis auto show. After Turnblad's death, the seven-year-old Chandler was listed in probate records as being valued at $50. Although Turnblad drove his cars himself at times, he also employed a chauffeur.

Turnblad's most exciting automobile adventure was undoubtedly his hair-raising trip to the St. Louis World's Fair from Minneapolis to St. Louis via Chicago in 1904 as part of the planned tour run. Turnblad, selected for the committee that planned the AAA trip, also participated in it. On the first day of the trip, Turnblad's Knox roadster had to be towed into town after it broke down. The next day, the brakes failed and the car rolled down a hill, either hitting or narrowly avoiding another car, depending on what account is believed. Near Dubuque, Iowa, a cylinder blew.[33]

Turnblad and the car eventually made it to St. Louis and apparently all his troubles were soon forgotten, as he told the Minneapolis Journal (Aug. 13, 1904), "I never enjoyed a trip so much in my life and was pleased to be able to finish three hours ahead of any of the other Twin City automobilists."

Describing the trip, he said:

"The run from the windy city to St. Louis was one of the pleasantest I ever made. The whole country for miles on

Turnblad was the first automobile owner in Minneapolis and he was asked to lead the procession of 13 cars journeying from the courthouse in downtown Minneapolis to the Lafayette Club on Lake Minnetonka in August of 1900.

Turnblad var den förste bilägaren i Minneapolis och han blev ombedd att leda en procession av 13 bilar från rådhuset i Minneapolis till Lafayette Club vid Lake Minnetonka i augusti år 1900.

either side of our route seemed to have heard of the autos and every farmyard was filled with country folk who had come, some of them long distances, to see us. They greeted us with cheers and waving of hats and threw flowers and fruits into the autos as they spun past."[34]

Reportedly, Christina and Lillian Turnblad rode along with Swan Turnblad on the journey to St. Louis, as they had accompanied him to Europe.

Notes: [32]*Minneapolis Journal*, April 10, 1900. [33]Information on Swan J. Turnblad's automobiles is taken from the writings of researcher and ASI member Robert R. Johnson, Minneapolis, Minnesota. [34]*Minneapolis Journal*, Aug. 13, 1904.

Swan and Christina Turnblad, second car from the left, were in a parade of automobiles at the Minnesota State Fair in 1900.

Swan och Christina Turnblad i andra bilen från vänster i en bilparad på Minnesota State Fair år 1900.

The Quiet Lives of Christina and Lillian Turnblad

Although much was written by and about Swan Turnblad during his lifetime, there is little record of Christina Turnblad's life independent of her husband's and not much more is known about their daughter. Christina reportedly liked art, though there is no evidence that she herself engaged in artistic pursuits, as Lillian did. Very little is known about the family's life together. A few Christmas gifts, such as a china puppy made by the Rörstrand Porcelain Company and given to Swan Turnblad from his wife and daughter, who had their names painted on the puppy's paws, have survived and are in the collection of the American Swedish Institute.

Christina died at the age of 68 in 1929. The *Svenska Amerikanska Posten's* obituary about her said she "died quietly and peacefully Friday 6 September, after patiently enduring a long illness...Nature herself cried tears of sorrow in the form of a fine rain when the remains of a beloved wife and mother were entrusted to the earth's silent place until resurrection morning."[35] She was buried in Lakewood Cemetery in Minneapolis.

The Turnblads' daughter, Lillian, was a shy person from all accounts and she, like her mother, left behind few clues to her life and her personality. She did keep scrapbooks of the family's travels and later of newspaper clippings, with notes on where the clippings appeared. The clippings included notices of art exhibits and receptions at the American Swedish Institute. Publisher of the *Posten* after her father died, she persevered until 1940, when the paper was sold. She apparently read Swedish, as the American Swedish Institute has several books in Swedish with her name inscribed in them.

Her interest in art apparently started early in life; she had art instruction and later often painted. One of her paintings is owned by the American Swedish Institute. It shows two young peasant women and a man in hiking clothes (wearing lederhosen and a Tyrolean-style hat, with a rucksack at his feet) chatting together in an alcove of a house. Also in the American Swedish Institute collection are several pieces of furniture, painted blue with hand-painted floral decorations, that are said to be the work of Lillian Turnblad.

Photographs of Lillian Turnblad later in life show a plain, stocky woman in unobtrusive dress. A far different Lillian is shown in a hand-tinted photograph of her wearing the ornately embroidered Värend folk dress from Småland, Sweden, with the sash embroidered with the year—1914—and the name of the king of Sweden, Gustav V.

Lillian Turnblad asked Sister Marie Teresa, an art teacher, to paint this posthumous oil portrait of her mother, Christina Turnblad.

Lillian Turnblad bad syster Marie Teresa, en teckningslärare, att måla detta postuma porträtt i olja av modern Christina.

In the photograph, taken in Minneapolis, she is attractive and pleasant looking. She is smiling slightly and appears slightly dreamy. She was then about 30 years old. The folk costume she wore in the photograph is in the permanent collection of the American Swedish Institute.

After her father's death, Lillian moved out of the apartment at 2615 Park and into a suite of rooms at The Academy of the Holy Angels, in Richfield, which is now a suburb of Minneapolis but then was mostly open countryside. She took some of her furniture with her, including an elaborate bedroom set. Lillian never became a Catholic, but she apparently felt at home at Holy Angels and had known at least one of the nuns previously. Several members of the Sisters of St. Joseph, now living in the order's retirement home in St. Paul, remember the woman they always referred to as "Miss Turnblad."

Sister Hubert Marie, who came to Holy Angels as a boarder in 1931, when it opened, and later became a nun, worked in the dining room as a waitress when Lillian Turnblad lived there. The arrangement of Lillian Turnblad living in the academy, Sister Hubert Marie said, was "unusual. She was a friend of Sister Caritas." Sister Caritas was in charge of the art department at Holy Angels and she and Lillian had known each other previously. "She had her own table in the corner of the dining room, facing away from the rest of us. She ate alone and she had her own pretty dishes. To us she seemed old. She had the chaplain's suite in the building, because there was no chaplain in residence. In the morning, after breakfast, the limo was waiting to pick her up and take her to work."

Sister Ellen, who was a young nun when Lillian lived at the academy, also remembers her. "She always wore very dark clothes. She was tall, a very gracious lady. I can still see her in chapel. She would go and sit in the very back. We loved her very much. I think she was very lonely after her parents died and she decided she didn't want to live alone." Sister Gregory and Lillian Turnblad would sometimes exchange a few words while Miss Turnblad waited for her limousine to arrive. "She was trained to be a lady," said Sister Gregory. "She read a lot of books."

Sister Gregory said, "She did not want any attention, she was very retiring." As for her appearance, Sister Gregory added, "She was ordinary looking. She wore no makeup."[36]

A letter written in 1937 by Sister Marie Teresa sheds a little more light on Lillian. "When I came from the College of St. Catherine where I had been head of the art department for more than twenty years, I found Miss Turnblad was living here [editor's note: at Holy Angels]. I knew her as a girl when I was instructor at St. Agatha's Conservatory and immediately we became the best of friends. She had me do her portrait from life and now I have an order for both her mother's and father's portraits but "they" are to be drawn and painted from photographs." The portraits now hang in the American Swedish Institute.

Sister Marie Teresa wrote the letter to the purchaser of an oriental rug that Lillian Turnblad—in gratitude to the nuns—had donated to Holy Angels

This oil portrait of Swan J. Turnblad, commissioned after his death by his daughter, Lillian, was painted by her friend, Sister Marie Teresa (nee Frances Mackey).

Detta porträtt i olja av Swan J. Turnblad beställdes efter hans död av hans dotter Lillian och målades av hennes vän, syster Marie Teresa (född Frances Mackey).

to sell in order to pay for some furnishings in the chapel at Holy Angels. Sister Marie Teresa wrote, "She and her mother prized the rug so highly and it makes her feel very happy that friends of mine are to own the only valuable object that she had left from all her father's wealth." The rug was bought in Constantinople, Turkey, in 1902 on one of the Turnblads' trips to Europe. Sister Marie Teresa, in a note received at the American Swedish Institute, said the Persian rug was made for Shah Abbas, the ruler of Persia (now called Iran) over a period of 45-50 years. The Shah died before it was finished and, due to the royal crown woven into it, the rug had to be sold abroad, and thus the Turnblads acquired it. According to Sister Marie Teresa, it was used in Mrs. Turnblad's second floor sitting room.[37]

Lillian Turnblad also had a small log cabin, with screens in place of windows, built by her chauffeur, Ben Hansen. Mr. Hansen built the walls and roof separately and assembled them on the convent grounds.[38] It was later demolished.

Lillian lived at the Academy until her last illness. She died in October of 1943 at the age of 59 and was buried at Lakewood Cemetery. The obituary in the *Minneapolis Tribune* of Oct. 20, 1943, said, "Miss Turnblad was a member of the executive committee of the (American Swedish) institute and devoted much of her time to its activities."[39]

The sisters at Holy Angels were aware of Lillian Turnblad's connection with the American Swedish Institute. "She loved that place," said Sister Gregory,

"but she was bitter about the trustee fight." [Editor's note: in 1940, she objected to a board vote to dismiss a *Posten* employee, as told in Emil Berglund's account in the American Swedish Institute Bulletin.]

It may have been this disagreement with the trustees of the American Swedish Institute that caused Lillian Turnblad to leave the net income from her estate to the Hennepin County Chapter of the American Red Cross "for the duration of the present war or wars, and for a period of one year after peace has been declared by the President of the United States."[40] After the war ceased, the trust was to benefit the Minneapolis Institute of Arts. She left none of her money to the American Swedish Institute, as many people expected her to do. At the time of her death, her estate was valued at nearly $300,000.

Her will instructs that the net income from her estate was to fund the "Christina N. and Swan J. Turnblad Memorial Fund as a memorial to my deceased parents" to be used "for the purchase, from time to time, for its permanent collection, works of Art of first class or highest quality."[41]

According to Richard L. Meyer, Director, Endowments and Planned Giving at the Minneapolis Institute of Arts, the net worth of the fund is now between $1 and $2 million. "It has been one of our significant art acquisition endowments, both historically and at the present time," said Meyer. "We have acquired some significant art works because of it."[42]

Lillian Turnblad's portrait was done by her friend, Sister Marie Teresa, who also lived at The Academy of the Holy Angels.

Lillian Turnblads porträtt målat av hennes vän syster Marie Teresa som också bodde på Academy of the Holy Angels.

The Academy of the Holy Angels, in Richfield, a suburb of Minneapolis, was Lillian Turnblad's home in her final years.

Academy of the Holy Angels i Richfield, en förort till Minneapolis, var Lillian Turnblads hem under hennes sista år.

Sweden's crown prince, Gustaf Adolf (later Gustaf VI Adolf), with eyeglasses in front row center, met with Lillian Turnblad and American Swedish Institute trustee Mike Holm during a visit to Minneapolis in 1938.

Sveriges kronprins Gustaf Adolf, senare Gustaf VI Adolf, med glasögon i första raden, träffade Lillian Turnblad och Mike Holm, en medlem i American Swedish Institutes styrelse, under ett besök i Minneapolis år 1938.

On Nov. 13, 1943, two of her cousins contested the will, but the court ruled that the will was valid on Dec. 2, 1943. The following year, the Executive Committee of what is now the American Swedish Institute announced that it had received a check for $13,423 from a claim filed against Lillian Turnblad's estate for losses incurred by the *Posten*, which Lillian Turnblad had promised to cover.

Notes: [35]*SAP*, Sept. 11, 1929. p. 20. [36]Interview with Sister Ellen Murphy, Sister Hubert Marie Weller, Sister Gregory Sanger, Sister Ann Thomasine Sampson, March, 1999, Bethany Home, St. Paul, Minnesota. [37]Letter from Sister Marie Teresa (née Frances Mackey), 1937. [38]Personal communication from Elinor Hansen Strot and Henry Hansen, children of Ben Hansen, chauffeur for Swan J. and Lillian Turnblad, to the author, May 20, 1999. [39]*Minneapolis Tribune*, Oct. 20, 1943. [40]She referred to World War II. [41]Last Will and Testament of Lillian Z. Turnblad. [42]Personal communication from Richard L. Meyer to the author, February, 1999.

Not Just Another Immigrant Newspaper

The shrunken and much-subdued *Svenska Amerikanska Posten* of which Lillian Turnblad became the publisher after Swan Turnblad's death was far different from the cheeky, robust newspaper over which her father reigned. Even so, the paper led an interesting life and died a respectable death,

from the journalistic equivalent of old age. Its rags-to-riches-to-dust story is the story of many other foreign language newspapers in the United States, as the tides of immigration ebbed and flowed.

Many of the approximately 350 Swedish-language

Turnblad had the last home of the Svenska Amerikanska Posten, at 500 South 7th Street in downtown Minneapolis, built in 1915.

Svenska Amerikanska Postens sista hem på South 7th Street 500 i Minneapolis.

TIMES BUILDING.

For some years before the 7th Street Posten building was constructed, the paper was produced in rented space at the Times Building at 207 6th Street South in Minneapolis.

Innan Postenfastigheten byggdes framställdes tidningen i hyrda lokaler i Times-byggnaden på 6th Street South 207 i Minneapolis.

newspapers that served the thousands of Swedish immigrants were of short duration, but several of them were published for many years. The number of Swedish-language newspapers published in the United States grew proportionately as the number of immigrants increased. There were 16 weekly Swedish-language newspapers in the United States in 1880; in 1890, 41 were being published. As Minnesota became home to many of the Swedish immigrants, it was not surprising that several Swedish-language newspapers were established there. By the time *Svenska Amerikanska Posten* began publishing in 1885, four other Swedish-language weekly newspapers were published in the state: *Skaffaren och Minnesota Stats Tidning, Svenska Folkets Tidning, Svenska Kristna Härolden* and *Missions-Bladet.*[43] The upstart *Posten* was to outlast all the others; it was published for 55 years.

Svenska Amerikanska Posten, the newspaper on which Swan Turnblad's fortune was built, began as a four-page journal advocating temperance. The first issue of the *SAP* declared it was "An independent Swedish Political Newspaper Devoted to the promotion of Temperance, Good Morals and the elevation of Society."[44]

Although founding details are hazy, the *Posten's* editor, N.P. Lind, who had studied theology in Sweden, apparently regarded himself as the leader of the 11 founders of the paper.[45] Turnblad was not one of the founders, although he was a strong supporter of the temperance movement. After moving to Minneapolis from Vasa, he worked as a typesetter for two Swedish-language news-

papers in Minneapolis—the *Minnesota Stats Tidning* and the *Svenska Folkets Tidning*—before joining *Svenska Amerikanska Posten.* Although he may have been hired as a typesetter, Turnblad was a stockholder in 1885 and is listed as manager of the *Posten* in the 1886 Dual City business directory. Somewhat contradictorily, Turnblad's occupation is shown as insurance agent in the 1886-1887 *Minneapolis City Directory.* At any rate, later editions of the *Minneapolis City Directory* show him employed by the *Posten.*[46]

Turnblad functioned differently than many of the other people associated with Swedish-language newspapers, several sources wrote. According to an early biographer, Chicago journalist C.F. Peterson, Turnblad, who was educated in the United States rather than Sweden, was "more American than Swedish, i.e. bolder and more energetic in his way of doing business, calmer and more calculating...which made him a 'great success as a businessman.' "[47]

Turnblad made the *Posten* a sounder business by contracting with local and national advertising agencies, who bought newspaper advertising space for their clients. He also increased the number of subscribers—thereby keeping the advertisers happy—by offering premiums, and he employed traveling subscription solicitors as well as the local subscription agents.[48] The *Posten* was not shy about tooting its horn: In the 1888 New Year's Greeting to subscribers, the paper declared that it had had 10,000 readers in 1887 and "next year we shall certainly reach 20,000 subscribers."[49] The editorial also announced that the expected increase in subscribers would allow the *Posten* to increase its size again.

To lure readers, the *Posten* offered many premiums at a discount with subscriptions: a world atlas, a retractable tape measure with a picture of Swan Turnblad on its casing, and a clock. The *Posten* made an effusive pitch for the clock: "This very smart and sought after clock...is surely the most beautiful article of its kind that has ever been made." The paper went on to say the clock was worth at least $5 but that subscribers could buy it for $2.50.[50]

The *Posten* at its inception was full of temperance-related material, as well as news from Sweden and Swedish America. It gradually turned away from its original goal of advocating temperance after Turnblad became the manager, although temperance still played a major role in the paper for a couple of decades.[51] Turnblad's brother, Magnus Turnblad, writing in a notebook now in the archives at the American Swedish Institute, said Swan Turnblad had declared that the *Posten's* temperance leanings had been a deterrent to the growth of the paper and that, to increase circulation, the paper would have to change its main thrust from temperance advocacy to broader interests.[52]

Although the newspaper continued to write about temperance in its New Year's greetings in the 1880s and prohibition remained a stated goal in a Jan. 3, 1893 editorial,[53] the facts show a different picture. The editorial of Dec. 24, 1889, said:

"All the issues of the day will be dealt with from an impartial point of view, and we will have an opportunity to deal with the cause of temperance in a better manner than was the case before. Only the latest and best news will be reported. The Sweden department will be given particular attention. Our serialized novels will if possible be even more thrilling and instructive than before. And poems, sketches and short stories will not be forgotten."[54]

The editorial message for the following year doesn't mention prohibition, but vows to "further the cause of our countrymen and of our program" and to "offer our readers editorial content of a magnitude equal to any Swedish-American newspaper."[55]

The paper's appearance in its early years was much like other newspapers of the era: type was small, headlines were seldom more than two columns wide and there was no color used. The temperance tone was evident throughout the paper, from editorials to poems to reprints of popular songs such as "Father, dear father, come home with me now/the clock on the mantel strikes one ..." about a child dragging a father home from a tavern.

Gradually, the temperance tone receded, ads became abundant and extravagant. Most of the ads were in Swedish, but some English began to creep in as the years went by. Still, it was evident that the paper served immigrants, as ads for steamship companies regularly touted passage from Sweden to America and land companies advertised cheap land. As with other newspapers of the era, truth-in-advertising was obviously not a

Among the many premiums used to tempt new Svenska Amerikanska Posten *subscribers was this "smart and sought after" clock.*

Bland de många premier som användes för att värva nya prenumeranter till Svenska Amerikanska Posten fanns denna "moderna och eftertraktade" klocka.

Magnus Martinson, left, owned and published the **Svenska Amerikanska Posten** *from 1920 to 1927. The woman at right is Hannah Swanson.*

Magnus Martinson, till vänster, ägde och utgav **Svenska Amerikanska Posten** *från 1920 till 1927. Kvinnan till höger hette Hannah Swanson.*

priority: one advertisement promised to grow hair on bald heads overnight; another praised the health-giving power of a so-called electric belt.

By 1904, the *Posten,* which was sold for five cents for a single copy, used color in some of its headlines and for design emphasis. There were also comic strips, many photos and separate sections for women, for those interested in gardening and for children. To celebrate the 1904 St. Louis World's Fair, the *Posten* ran an elaborate section on the fair and also on the cities of Minneapolis and St. Paul, perhaps to give away as souvenirs at the fair. The title page of this section, a full page, shows the Swedish building at the fair and the Minnesota building on a background of a brilliant blue, surrounded by an elaborate border with Viking motifs.[56] However, many of these features disappeared later, and the *SAP* assumed a more sedate look.[57]

Turnblad was constantly promoting his paper. The Jan. 19, 1904, issue carried a prominent box, bordered in red, with a red headline that bragged: "Issue number 1,000!" The blurb went on to say that, from a sickly start, the paper had become the largest and most widely circulated Swedish newspaper in America. At its height, circulation was more than 50,000, according to journalism professor and author Ulf Jonas Björk.

The *Posten* was not a frivolous paper, however, despite its play for subscribers. Editorials discussed the major questions of the day, which very often had nothing to do with Swedish America. Likewise, the letters to the editor, under a standing headline called *Folkets Röst* (The People's Voice) came from readers who wrote on a variety of things, including their personal lives and topics that were timely. The feature was so popular, in fact, that editors could not run all the letters.

Consequently, restrictions were put on submissions and specific topics for correspondents to discuss were selected.[58]

Despite the fact that Turnblad employed editors, it is obvious that he took a strong interest in the editorial workings of the paper. He corresponded with contributors to the *Posten,* sometimes mentioning personal as well as business matters. In one letter to a *Posten* writer, Turnblad mentions the death of his dog, Toby.[59] Toby seems to have been a fixture at the *Posten* office. In the 1960 memoir recalling her days working handling subscriptions at the newspaper, Hilda Benson wrote:

> "Mr. Turnblad had a pet, his inseparable companion (an Airedale dog) named Toby. Toby had a bell attached to his collar around his neck, so beware, when we heard this bell, we knew our boss was near. Toby had a special bath tub in the basement of the Posten Bldg., I can picture Mr. Turnblad with a towel over his arm and Toby by his side going for his daily bath."[60]

Hilda Benson also mentions Turnblad's strict rules: women employees were to wear black, never white, stockings. When Benson presented him with the money for subscriptions, he wanted it in strict order:

> "Each morning I would bring the money to Mr. Turnblad's office and if I did not have the money neatly stacked with the correct face up, from the $20 bill on the bottom to the penny on top of the pile, I was asked to bring it back to my desk and correct it."[61]

Turnblad valued his employees, however, as Benson attested in writing about his reaction to the death of her father, who had been the foreman of the *Posten's* composing room: "When my Dad was killed in 1928, Mr. Turnblad was very upset and wanted to discontinue printing the Posten. I can remember him coming to our home to pay his respects. The first thing he said was 'Why didn't I praise him while he lived. I can not go on without him.'"[62]

Turnblad did go on without her father, however, and remained the publisher of the *SAP* until his death in 1933, with the exception of the years from 1920 to 1927. Turnblad had sold the paper to Magnus Martinson in 1920 and city directories during that seven-year period show Turnblad with no occupation. The *SAP* did not thrive under Martinson and he declared the paper bankrupt in 1927. Turnblad formed a company, bought it back and remained the publisher to the end of his days.[63]

Much of Turnblad's time and money over the years was taken up with a series of lawsuits by disgruntled former *Posten* stockholders. The siege of lawsuits began in 1908 when Isaac Ekberg, a former stockholder, and others filed a suit against Turnblad. Later suits by Ekberg also named the *Posten* itself and Christina Turnblad.

The anger among former stockholders apparently stemmed from Turnblad's apparent undervaluing of the stock, which led many stockholders to sell their stock to him. Ellen Stead, who brought suit against Turnblad in 1911, claimed, according to a *Minneapolis Journal* article, that shares of stock worth $10 in 1885 were now worth $8,000. The Ekberg suit—which sought nearly $1 million from

Turnblad—was decided in favor of Turnblad in District Court, a decision later overturned on appeal to the Minnesota Supreme Court, which said the case must be retried. On Nov. 25, 1911, the stockholders and Turnblad reached an agreement, giving the stockholders $20,000 and a deed to property in Pine County, Minnesota.

That was not the end of litigation for Turnblad, however. His brother, Magnus, who had been at his side or in close correspondence with him during the lawsuit years, also sued Turnblad, his wife and daughter, and the *Posten* in 1914, demanding an account of the *Posten's* financial records. There was no further record of this suit.[64]

Turnblad's last years as publisher of the *Posten* may have been relatively tranquil, compared to the earlier tumultuous years. It is not known whether Lillian Turnblad was being groomed as her father's successor. Hilda Benson's memoir does mention her presence in the *Posten* office, although seemingly not in an executive position:

> "She [Lillian Turnblad] used to appear once in a while and ask the girls if she could be of any assistance. Her hair was combed in a knot on top of her head with a pencil stuck in it, most always a white blouse and a long black skirt in addition always a black sateen apron, a scissors tied to a string which was tied around her waist."[65]

Lillian Turnblad did assume the publisher role, however, and visited the paper every day. The *Posten* also had editors, in addition to Turnblad as publisher. Gradually, as the number of Swedish speakers diminished over the years, the *Posten* grew smaller in size and had fewer advertisers. By the time it was sold, in 1940, it was down to eight pages, with only a few ads.

Lillian Turnblad was faithful to her father's memory even to the last issue. While the information that the paper had been sold was given only in a couple of sentences on page one, Lillian and editor Carl "Vidar" Mattson each wrote a farewell editorial on page two. Lillian thanked readers for their faithfulness and said the paper had never deviated from its significant mission of preserving Swedish culture abroad. She wrote, "At the same time, the newspaper has also had another mission, to help Swedish immigrants adjust to the new circumstances they encountered in this country."

She continued, "Every paper has its own stamp and Svenska Amerikanska Posten has [had] its...The paper's owner and publisher for a span of 40 years, Mr. Swan J. Turnblad, decided right from the beginning that the newspaper should work on behalf of piety, temperance, and the uplifting of people and it has never deserted that aim. At the same time, it has sought to further Swedish culture here in this country and to be a good and reliable newspaper."

She concluded: "To all our readers, we send forth a heartfelt thanks for the years that have gone before. There are subscribers who have had this paper for many, many years. And we know that they will miss it. But they will get another good and well-edited newspaper in its stead—Svenska Amerikanaren Tribunen."[66]

Notes: [43]Ulf Jonas Björk, "Proud to be a Yellow Journal: *Svenska Amerikanska Posten,* An Immigrant Newspaper with American Accents," presented at the Swedish Life in the Twin Cities Conference, St. Paul, Minnesota, 1996, pp. 1-3. [44]Hammerstrom chronology. [45]Björk, p. 4. [46]Hammerstrom chronology. [47]Björk, p. 6, quoting C.F. Peterson, *Sverige i Amerika: Kulturhistoriska och biografiska teckningar* (Chicago: The Royal Star Company, 1898). [48]Ibid. [49]*SAP,* Jan. 6, 1888. [50]*SAP,* April 12, 1905. p. 14. [51]Björk, p. 6. [52]Ibid., p. 7 [53]Ibid. [54]Ibid. [55]Ibid. [56]*SAP,* June 21, 1904. [57]Ulf Jonas Björk *Folkets Röst, "The Pulse of the Public": Svenska Amerikanska Posten* and Reader Letters, 1907-1911, the *Swedish American Historical Quarterly* Vol. 50, number 2, April 1999, p. 12. [58]Ibid., p. 6. [59]Letter to Johan G.R. Banér, April 5, 1929, Johan G.R. Banér Papers, Bentley Historical Library, University of Michigan. [60]Benson, Hilda, "My Memoir of *Svenska Amerikanska Posten,*" Nov. 25, 1960, in the ASI archives, 2. [61]Ibid. [62]Ibid. [63]Hammerstrom chronology. [64]Ibid.; also, Lawrence Hammerstrom, "The Swedish American Publishing Company Stockholders' Lawsuit Against Swan J. Turnblad," in *Swedish American Historical Society Quarterly,* Jan. 1984. [65]Benson, p. 1. [66]*SAP,* Sept. 11, 1940, p. 2.

Swan J. Turnblad, shown at his desk, oversaw the expansion of the fledgling Svenska Amerikanska Posten to its height as the Swedish-language paper with the largest circulation in the United States at one time.

Swan J. Turnblad, här vid sitt skrivbord, övervakade expansionen av den lilla Svenska Amerikanska Posten till dess ställning som den svenskspråkiga tidning som en tid hade den största spridningen i Förenta Staterna.

The Last Years and the Founding of the American Swedish Institute

One of several certificates of gratitude to Swan Turnblad for establishing what is now known as the American Swedish Institute.

Ett av de många tacksamhetsbevis som Swan Turnblad fick för att han etablerade vad som idag kallas American Swedish Institute.

Swan Turnblad worked at the newspaper well past normal retirement age. On his 70th birthday, in 1930, great notice was taken of this anniversary in the local papers. The *Minneapolis Tribune* of Oct. 7, 1930, said that Turnblad had planned to get up early and go to Vasa to visit his mother's grave. However, the article noted, weather prevented him from making the drive to Vasa and he spent the day at his desk.[67]

Before his 70th birthday, however, Turnblad had ended years of indecision about what to do with his magnificent mansion, which had stood empty for several years. We may never know whether he had planned to give the house to the Swedish community for years, as he claimed in newspaper accounts, or whether he finally decided that the taxes were too high or that it cost too much to keep it up. In any case, he and his wife and their daughter, Lillian, had apparently decided to donate it to the Swedish community before Christina Turnblad's death in the fall of 1929. Turnblad had been talking with the Swedish Consul, Nils Jaenson, since 1925 about donating his house to a Swedish institution.

Initially, Turnblad insisted that $100,000 be raised in order to maintain the house. Jaenson balked at this and negotiations dragged on. Finally, Turnblad decided to donate the house to a Swedish-American foundation. Sweden's Crown Prince Gustaf Adolf responded warmly by letter on July 22, 1929, thanking Turnblad and promising to be the institute's patron, provided Turnblad committed himself to the donation and if sufficient funding were found to ensure the maintenance.

Final negotiations were interrupted by Christina Turnblad's death in September, 1929. After her death, Turnblad agreed to also donate the *SAP* itself as well as the *Posten* building. The charter establishing the "American Institute of Swedish Arts, Literature, and Science," now called the American Swedish Institute, from these donations was registered with the Secretary of State in Minnesota on Nov. 30, 1929.[68]

In newspaper interviews, Turnblad said he had planned to give the house to the Swedish community for many years.

"Many persons may have wondered what a small family like ours, a family which had not great social ambitions, wanted with so big a home. Perhaps they can guess now."

"I had this idea in mind when I first began to build the home. I wanted it to endure for a hundred thousand years. And I wanted to have it so arranged that it might easily be converted to its later uses."[69]

Turnblad also said, "It has been my lifelong ambition to foster and preserve Swedish culture in America. I hold dear many things that are Swedish—although I am an American now—and it seems to me to be desirable for both countries if some of the products of Swedish culture might be shown here."[70]

Turnblad remained as publisher of the *SAP* and he was also on the board of directors of the newly formed institute. The house was first opened to the public on August 14, 1930.

Swan Turnblad's final illness was followed closely by the local newspapers. He had heart disease and died in the early morning hours of May 17, 1933. He was buried beside his wife, Christina, in Lakewood Cemetery in Minneapolis. Many people from all walks of life attended his funeral. Among the tributes to him were poems written in Swedish. A bouquet of flowers, picked by a friend the previous summer in the hills near Turnblad's home at Tubbamåla and laid on the casket, was a final reminder of Sweden. Obituaries praising him appeared in many newspapers. The *Minneapolis Tribune* wrote:

"In Swan J. Turnblad was to be found the embodiment of many of the finest things which one nationality has contributed to the American scene...As the publisher of the *Svenska Amerikanska Posten* over a period of some 30 years, as the patron of the arts and sciences, and donor of the American Institute of Swedish Arts, Literature and Science, Mr. Turnblad was the exponent of that

which was best in the cultural tradition of his nationality...In his death not only his nationality but the state have been deprived of a valued leader."[71]

Notes: [67]*Minneapolis Tribune*, Oct. 7, 1930. [68]This abbreviated account of the establishment of the American Swedish Institute is taken from "Swan Johan Turnblad and the Founding of the American Swedish Institute," by Nils William Olsson and Lawrence G. Hammerstrom, (presented at the Swedish Life in the Twin Cities Conference, St. Paul, Minnesota 1996). [69]*Minneapolis Tribune*, Dec. 15, 1929. p. 2. [70]Lilly Lorénzen, "The Institute: A Short History," *American Swedish Institute Bulletin*, Vol. 9, No. 3, Autumn 1954. p.4. [71]*Minneapolis Tribune*, May 18, 1933, p. 12.

The Swedish Cultural Society in America awarded Swan Turnblad this certificate for his work in establishing the American Swedish Institute.

Swan Turnblad fick detta diplom av Svenska Kulturförbundet i Amerika för sitt arbete med grundandet av American Swedish Institute.

The view of Turnblad's "castle" through its wrought-iron gates is imposing.

En imponerande syn: Turnblads "slott" genom grindarna.

The "Castle"

Tall, ornate iron gates swing back to admit the public to the grand mansion that is now the American Swedish Institute. Some call the building "the Swedish castle." It is not only a center for Swedish-American culture, but a grand testimony to the power of the American dream.

No one knows when and where Swan Turnblad got the idea for building his house. It may be that he was impressed by the chateaus in France during his travels or possibly he had seen grand manor houses in southern Sweden as a boy. In any case, he may have long harbored the idea of building a marvelous house on one of the young city's best streets. Accordingly, after an earlier abortive attempt to build near Loring Park, he bought six city lots between Park and Oakland Avenues, south of 26th Street, in 1903.

Park Avenue was a fashionable street for affluent Minneapolis families, who built large, impressive homes. Not only did the city's elite live on Park Avenue, but it was the first street in the city to be paved. Among the other mansions on or near Park Avenue were those owned by the Pillsbury, McKnight, Peavey, Bell, Sawyer, Cargill and Phelps families. Few of their impressive homes remain today.

Three architectural firms submitted designs for the house to Turnblad. They were W.H. Dennis of Minneapolis, Frank G. Cauffman of Philadelphia and Boehme and Cordella of Minneapolis. Turnblad chose the elaborate, chateau-like design submitted by Christopher A. Boehme (1865-1916) and Victor Cordella (1872-1937). The young architects (Cordella was barely in his 30s and Boehme not yet 40) drew up blueprints in 1904; construction started the same year and was finished in 1908.

The silhouette of the mansion is intricate, with a tower, steeply pitched roofs, gables, gargoyles and a long, railed porch, whose central, roofed entry is supported by stone columns. The building is not symmetrical; on the north end is the three-story, three-sided bay construction that gives the first floor salon, the second floor "glass" room and the third story weaving room their grace and light. On the opposite side of the house, looking like an illustration from a book of fairy tales, is the tower, with its conical roof topped with a copper figure. The mansion was built of light gray Indiana limestone.

Around the back is the former carriage house, also built of the same material. Notice the horse's head projecting over the entrance; reportedly it was carved free-hand by Herman Schlink, who did all the exterior carving on the mansion and the carriage house. Schlink, according to one account, had

The lion is a recurring image in the house exterior; lions on the south and west sides of the roof double as waterspouts.

Lejon förekommer ofta i exteriören; dessa på södra och västra sidan av taket fungerar som stuprännor.

Fanciful beasts serve as waterspouts (top) and elaborate gargoyles (below) adorn the exterior of the house.

Fantasifulla djur fungerar som stuprör (överst) och groteska stuprännstutar pryder exteriören (underst).

packed his tools to leave and Turnblad called him back to carve the horse's head over the carriage house. Schlink also carved the lions' heads in the gables and was told by Turnblad to make them as grotesque as he could, according to Elmer Albinson.[72]

On the exterior wall of the passageway that now links the carriage house with the main house is a stained glass window that was in the former *Svenska Amerikanska Posten* office in downtown Minneapolis; when the office building was torn down, the window was installed in the connecting passageway.

In addition to the main entrance at the front of the mansion, the office entrance through the carriage house and the recently installed door leading directly into the auditorium, there was an entrance on the north side of the building. The gate is still there, but the door, which led to the first floor den, now the ASI Museum Shop, is sealed.

The house has 33 rooms; many are small and not open to the public. There are three stories, plus a lower level and an attic. Some spaces that are designated on the heating blueprints (the architects' blueprints are not in the ASI collection), such as the darkroom on the third floor, were never built. In the interior of the richly decorated house, certain motifs occur repeatedly, lions and winged cherubs and dolphins being the most obvious. Throughout the house, the exquisitely carved woodwork, the beautiful porcelain *kakelugnar* (tile stoves), and the intricate plasterwork on the ceilings invite inspection.

In the years since Turnblad donated his house to the Swedish-American community, it has welcomed many visitors, from average folks who may or may not have any connection to Sweden to H.R.H. Carl XVI Gustaf, King of Sweden. Other prominent visitors include former President Dwight Eisenhower, Swedish film director Jan Troell, Swedish author Astrid Lindgren and actors Max von Sydow and Ann-Margret. Whatever their station, visitors never forget whose house this was: Swan J. Turnblad left his literal stamp on it. In the entryway, the entwined initials S.J.T. are carved into the doorframe. In the dining room, every piece of the Rörstrand dinner service has his full name and address, 2600 Park Avenue, on the back. Several furniture pieces also have his initials carved into them and several large blue-and-white porcelain urns also bear his initials.

Notes: [72]Elmer Albinson "The Institute's Stone Carvings" *American Swedish Institute Bulletin*, Vol. X, No. 1, Summer, 1955, p. 5.

Turnblad's "castle" appeared to be completed when trees were being planted on 26th Street around 1909.

Turnblads slott verkade vara färdigbyggt då träd planterades på 26th Street omkring år 1909.

Swan Turnblad's name and address is on each piece of the Rörstand china (left) and his initials are entwined on a porcelain urn.

Swan Turnblads namn och adress finns på varje del av Rörstrandsservisen (till vänster) och hans sammanflätade initialer på en porslinsurna.

The First Floor

The Grand Hall

Visitors step from the entryway into the soaring space of the Grand Hall. Two stories high, the room is paneled and embellished in burnished, reddish-brown African mahogany. The fireplace mantel, also two stories high and carved from the same beautiful wood, is the room's focus point.

Well-known sculptor Albin Polasek designed and carved the fireplace mantel and decorations and the figures that flank it. White onyx surrounds the fireplace opening. On either side of the fireplace are two male figures, which Polasek reportedly called "barbarians." The figures bear urns on their heads and they wear only animal skins. The one nearest the stairs wears a wolfskin; the other is draped in a sheepskin.

Above the mantel itself, with its richly carved garlands, is a working clock with a maiden leaning in on it from either side. The maiden closest to the stairs represents night; her eyes are closed, her right hand holds the sun down against her hip and her left arm is held high, clutching the moon. The other maiden signifies day, with her eyes open and butterflies perched in her hair.

The second story of the fireplace includes a full-length figure of a Viking, added later, which is set inside a pillared enclosure. The entire fireplace structure is topped with a bust, apparently also of a Viking.

At the foot of the staircase leading to the landing are two carved winged lions. They have often been referred to as "griffins." However, the mythological beasts known as griffins have the head and wings of an eagle and the body of a lion, whereas the animals on either side of the stairs have lion heads as well as bodies; only the wings are remindful of griffins. The paws of the creatures are extended, perhaps to signify welcome to guests.

The walls of the Grand Hall serve as exhibit space for paintings by Swedish and Swedish-American artists. The works of art are changed from time to time. On either side of the fireplace are huge porcelain urns, decorated near the top with sculpted elephant heads, complete with tusks. They were made at the Rörstrand Porcelain Company in Sweden and purchased by Swan Turnblad early in the 20th century. They normally serve as planters.

Remember to look up at the ceiling above the Grand Hall. The cherubs bearing garlands are sculpted in plaster. Originally painted in colors, the plaster sculptures were at one time repainted white like the rest of the ceiling. In the 1980s, the

sculptures were repainted in colors typical of the era during which the house was built and a frieze was stenciled just below the ceiling.

The Salon

Many grand houses built in the first part of the 20th century included a salon, an upscale version of the traditional parlor. The Salon in the Turnblad mansion, in the front of the building, is a rectangular room that is bright with light. The east wall has several windows and on the north side of the

room is a graceful three-sided bay window. The Salon is decorated in the so-called Rococo Revival style, characterized by fancifully curved shapes and ornamental shell carvings.

As in the Grand Hall, the plaster work on the ceiling of the Salon has been repainted to replicate colors used during the time the house was constructed. The painting was done by Gertrude Gump, who also painted the Breakfast Room. A long, narrow mirror is attached to an interior wall.

Left, the fireplace in the Grand Hall is carved of African mahogany.

Till vänster: Den öppna spisen i entréhallen är snidad i mahogny från Afrika.

Right, visitors should remember to look up at the ceilings in the house; this polychromed ceiling is above the Grand Hall.

Till höger: Besökare får inte glömma att titta på taken i huset. Detta mångfärgade tak är i entréhallen.

The salon, a light and airy room, is used for temporary exhibits.

Salongen, ett ljust och luftigt rum, används för temporära utställningar.

Even the thermostats in Turnblad's house were ornate.

Till och med termostaterna i Turnblads hus var utsirade.

A specially woven wool carpet, with colors in harmony with the ceiling colors, is on the floor. Doors lead from the Salon to the Grand Hall and to the Den (now the ASI Museum Shop).

During the Turnblads' stay in the house, the Salon was probably used very seldom, if at all. Now, the American Swedish Institute uses the room for occasional exhibits and presentations.

The Den

A door off the Grand Hall leads to the Den, a Moorish fantasy of a room. Dens were common features when the mansion was built and the Moorish (or Arabic) style of decor was very popular early in the 20th century. The Den, now used as the American Swedish Institute Museum Shop, has been changed greatly over the years and has partially been restored to resemble its original state.

The ceramic tile stove—or *kakelugn*—is one of 11 similar stoves in the house. This one, manufactured at the Rörstrand Porcelain Company in Sweden in 1895, is perhaps the most colorful of those in the mansion. It is pink, blue and yellow, with gold trim, and has a brass door. Although all the stoves are in working order, they were seldom if ever used, as the mansion had central heating.

However, the Den's stove has been used, as shown by a photo of a fire in it. Throughout the house are ornate thermostats.

The *kakelugn* design is echoed in the elaborate, all-over geometric ceiling design. The design was probably chosen from *Ornamentets Bok,* a book of architectural samples that Turnblad owned, and in which he had written tentative design choices. It is now in the American Swedish Institute archives. The book contains patterns in the Moorish section that are identical to those used in the Den. The ceiling was repainted in 1986 by Marvin A. Anderson and Curt Pederson, specialists in historic restoration, who uncovered the original colors and matched them.

Unfortunately, the wooden pillars and wooden frieze carvings that were part of the room's original decor were removed in the 1940s. In their place is a Moorish-inspired stenciled wall design. An elaborate Moorish-style chandelier that once hung in the Den was given to the Zuhrah Shrine Temple, across 26th Street from the Turnblad mansion, by Lillian Turnblad in the 1940s.

The Dining Room

The most elaborately carved of the mansion's rooms is the Dining Room. It is located off the Grand Hall. At one end of the room is a bow window that extends nearly from floor to ceiling. The walls, ceiling and massive fireplace have intricate carvings of flowers, fruit and wreaths in oak and bleached Honduran mahogany. The wall panels and the furniture were designed and carved by Ulrich Steiner.

The Den—now the American Swedish Institute Museum Shop—was influenced by the Moorish style popular around the beginning of the century.

Sällskapsrummet, nu American Swedish Institutes presentbutik, var inspirerat av den moriska stil som var populär i början av seklet.

The Dining Room is the most extensively carved room in the house.

Matsalen har mer träsniderier än något annat rum i huset.

The Dining Room's built-in sideboard has intricate carving and both convex and concave glass doors.

Matsalens väggfasta byffé har konstfulla sniderier och både konvexa och konkava glasdörrar.

Closeup of the sideboard shows the shell motif and curved glass door.

Närbild på byffén visar snäck-motiv och bågformig glasdörr.

The fireplace is between two carved wooden benches. Serving as decorative supports (caryatids) for the mantelpiece are two female figures, also carved in wood. The face of the fireplace itself is green marble from Kolmården, Sweden. One of the carved wreaths is centered in the mantel over the fireplace. Inside the Della Robbia-style circle are several figures that represent the legend of a maiden being taken "into the mountain" by a troll-like figure. This ancient legend of a young girl lured inside a mountain by mythic creatures, never to return, is told in most Scandinavian countries. The image of the wreath is now used as the official seal of the American Swedish Institute.

A second carved wreath is on the ceiling above the dining room table. The table, which expands to seat 24 people, is believed to have been carved in place by Steiner. When it is extended, it conforms to the shape of the room, with one end curved to match the curve of the bow window and the other end squared off. Steiner also carved the beautiful built-in sideboard, which has both convex and concave glass doors. The sideboard features wedge-shaped drawers, rounded on the end, on either side. The shape of the drawers conserves space.

The porcelain dinner service made for the Turnblads is on display in the Dining Room. The pattern, called *Empire,* is white edged in a royal blue band and gold trim. It was made by Sweden's Rörstrand Porcelain Company. Each piece of the service bears Swan Turnblad's name and address on the back.

On the dining room floor is the original wool rug, which was woven to complement the designs of the room's carvings. The rug has deep, jewel-like tones and is in good condition.

The Breakfast Room

The Breakfast Room, which adjoins the Dining Room, is a great contrast to the Dining Room in style and decoration. It is decorated and furnished as an 18th century Swedish manor house would have been. The Breakfast Room's focal point is the white, gold trimmed *kakelugn,* one of two with mirrors in the house. The style of the *kakelugn,* made by the Rörstrand Porcelain Company of Stockholm, is Rococo Revival. Here, compared to the Dining Room, there is relatively little carving. The walls are painted white, with delicate color trim. In the small room is furniture in the 18th century Gustavian style. "Gustavian," a Swedish modification of furniture made in the style of the French "Sun King," Louis XIV, is named after the Swedish King Gustav III. Original Gustavian furniture was made from 1770 to 1810.

A recent acquisition is the 18th century Mora clock. The long-case, white-painted clock is typical of the curvy timepieces made in Mora, in the Swedish province of Dalarna. On the wall is a portrait of an unknown woman, painted by Gustaf Hesselius (1682-1755). Hesselius, who was born and trained as an artist in Sweden, emigrated to Delaware in 1712 and became the first nationally known Swedish-American painter.

A door to the Breakfast Room from the first-floor pantry of the house is no longer used. The kitchen

area, now used as storage and work space for the staff of the American Swedish Institute Museum Shop, is not open to the public. A hallway, a butler's pantry and a small lounge for the original staff of the house are also used for storage.

The Music Room

The Music Room was created with concerts and recitals in mind. Master woodcarver Ulrich Steiner carved lyres on the massive square wooden pillars, an indication of the room's purpose. On the ceiling of an alcove of the main music room are plaster reliefs of musical instruments. Reportedly, the acoustics are excellent.

The light Breakfast Room, a contrast to the dark Dining Room, is decorated in the Gustavian style to resemble an 18th century manor house in Sweden.

Det ljusa frukostrummet, en kontrast till den mörka matsalen, är inredd i gustaviansk stil för att likna en svensk herrgård på 1700-talet.

This 18th century "Mora" clock was made in Dalarna, Sweden.

Denna moraklocka från 1700-talet är tillverkad i Dalarna.

Around the room and on the fireplace are a total of 52 winged cherubs, carved in Honduran mahogany. The pillars support carved friezes that circle the room and on which the cherubs hold carved garlands in their hands. The cherubs face each other in pairs. As all are hand-carved, no two are exactly identical, although there seem to be four different styles. Each style has a different posture and a different wing placement. Larger cherubs adorn the mirrored fireplace. One of Steiner's descendants reportedly said that Steiner said he hoped he would never have to carve another cherub in his life after he finished the Music Room.

The ceiling and walls in the Music Room, which had originally been painted white, were painted in polychrome colors in 1980-1981 by restorers Marvin A. Anderson and Curt Pederson.

The wool rug, on which the mahogany Steinway grand piano stands, was ordered by Swan Turnblad in the early 1900s. Reportedly it was made of wool from Sweden but had to be woven by Austrian looms because the looms in Sweden were too small.

The Music Room is adorned with 52 winged cherubs, created by master woodcarver Ulrich Steiner, who reportedly said he hoped he would never have to carve another cherub after he finished the last one.

Musikrummet pryds av 52 bevingade keruber, skapade av mästersnidaren Ulrich Steiner som när han hade gjort den sista keruben sade att han hoppades att han aldrig skulle behöva göra en till.

The winged cherubs in the music room have several different poses.

De bevingade keruberna i musikrummet har många olika poser.

The Stairway Landing

The Visby Window

At the head of the stairway leading from the Grand Hall is the magnificent "Visby Window," with its glowing colors and amazing detail. The window is a copy of a painting by Swedish artist Carl Gustaf Hellqvist (1851-1890) titled "Valdemar Atterdag Levying Contributions on Visby." The original painting is in the National Museum in Stockholm, Sweden.

The scene portrays an historic event that took place in 1361 A.D. in Visby, a town on the island of Gotland in the Baltic Sea. Gotland was at that time a member of the Hanseatic League, a trade association that might be regarded as a forerunner of the European Community of today. The Danish King, Valdemar Atterdag, threatened to destroy the city of Visby and its citizens unless they surrendered their valuables to him. At the right of the window, the red-bearded king is shown seated on a dais in the Visby town square. His name is visible on an overhead canopy.

All around the king are the people of Visby, reluctantly bringing their treasures to be dumped into huge wooden barrels in front of him. A soldier with a pikestaff grabs one man by the arm, pulling him toward the barrels. It is clear from the expressions on their faces that the townspeople are resentful of the king's demands. The facial features and expressions, the clothing worn by the citizens and the objects and buildings in the square are minutely detailed.

The magnificent "Visby Window," on the main stairway landing, has great detail as well as glowing colors. The window is a copy of a painting by Swedish artist Carl Gustaf Hellqvist titled "Valdemar Atterdag Levying Contributions on Visby."

Det magnifika Visbyfönstret på huvudtrappans avsats har såväl underbara detaljer som lysande färger. Fönstret är en kopia av en målning av den svenske konstnären Carl Gustaf Hellqvist kallad Valdemar Atterdag brandskattar Visby.

View of the copper-roofed solarium from the exterior. It sits atop the portico over the original driveway.

Vy från utsidan av solariets koppartak. Det ligger över den ursprungliga uppfartsvägens pelargång.

The window was created by fusing oil-based enamel on hand-blown glass. The hundreds of pieces of glass were cut out and put together much like a gigantic jigsaw puzzle. The pieces are held together with lead caming. The process of fusing the glass with color gives the window colors of unusual brilliance and transparency, especially when the window is backlit by sunlight. The window was made in 1908 by the Neuman and Vogel Glass Company of Stockholm, Sweden. The best view of the window can be obtained from the second floor balcony.

The Solarium

Like many impressive houses of the same era, the Turnblad mansion has a Solarium. The structure juts out over the driveway, providing shelter for passengers getting in and out of cars and using a side door in the house. The Solarium has glass walls on three sides and a copper roof. A built-in bench wraps around the interior walls. The Solarium is entered by doors directly under the Visby Window on the stairway landing. Flanking the doors are two stained glass windows depicting armored medieval guards, swords in hand, that reflect the Visby scene in the window. The Solarium has not been restored and is not currently open to the public.

Did the Turnblads Live in the House?

One of the questions that visitors to the American Swedish Institute most frequently ask is whether the Turnblad family actually lived in the house. The answer is a qualified yes. According to research done by American Swedish Institute member Lawrence Hammerstrom, Swan Turnblad is listed in the *Minneapolis City Directory* as living in the house at 2600 Park Avenue as early as 1905 (but probably actually 1908, and also in 1920-1921 and in 1923-1926, although the 1922 city directory shows him residing at 500 South 7th Street in downtown Minneapolis (the office of *Svenska Amerikanska Posten*). The U.S. census records of 1910 and 1920 show Turnblad at 2600 Park Avenue.

In addition, the *Minneapolis Tribune* reported that 500 people attended the Aero Club open house at the house at 2600 Park Avenue in 1921. Several sources say that the Turnblads used only the second story of the house when they were in residence; *Posten* employee Hilda Benson wrote, in her memoir, that the Turnblads spent days in the house on Park Avenue and slept in their apartment over the *Posten* office.

The Second Floor

The largest rooms on the second floor are arranged around the perimeter of the balcony. From the balcony visitors can look down into the Grand Hall. Just off the balcony, near the elevator, is a smaller series of rooms that are now used by the staff of the American Swedish Institute and are not open to the public. Originally, these rooms included a workroom and a bedroom for the seamstress, who would stay for as long as it took to sew new garments. A stairway, much narrower than the grand staircase that leads to the Visby Window, leads to the second and third floors from the Grand Hall. On a stairway landing is a half bath, with original fixtures. It is open to the public.

The ceiling in the balcony area, which can be seen from the Grand Hall below, was polychromed in the 1980s by Marvin A. Anderson and Curt Pederson. The painting was done by erecting a platform and scaffold across the balcony railing.

Although the first floor has been restored to some semblance of what it may have been like during the Turnblads' residence, the public rooms on the second floor are primarily used for exhibits.

On the heating blueprint, five of the rooms on the second floor, including the Den, are designated as

In this photo, taken in the 1930s in the Library, portieres hang in the doorways.

På detta foto, taget i biblioteket på 30-talet, hänger det draperier i dörröppningarna.

55

The dark-green kakelugn in the Library depicts a 16th century tale.

Den mörkgröna kakelugnen i biblioteket skildrar en sägen från 1500-talet.

The Den is a cozy, book-lined room adjoining the Library.

Läsrummet är ett trevligt litet rum med bokskåp intill biblioteket.

"chambers," rather than rooms for specific purposes or persons to use.

The Library

On the second floor, entered off the balcony, is the Library, a warm, inviting room in which Swan Turnblad housed his own collection of books. The spines of many of the books are stamped in gold and add a richness to the room. Both the built-in bookcases and the paneled walls in the Library are made of bleached American walnut, a wood native to the American Midwest. Whether Turnblad spent much time in the room is not known, but it is a room that could surely keep any book-lover happy. The wooden library table in the center of the room is Turnblad's own.

In addition to books from Turnblad's own collection, the Library now contains many other books and bound periodicals in both Swedish and English.

At one end of the room is the dark-green *kakelugn*, with its center relief depicting the German merchant Jacob Fugger and Emperor Charles V, King of both Spain and the Netherlands. The event depicted happened in Augsburg in approximately 1520 A.D. Fugger had lent the Emperor money and Fugger, to show how rich he was, is depicted burning the signed notes from the Emperor that promised to pay him back. The fire in the fireplace, so the story goes, was built of cinnamon sticks, which were extremely expensive and was another way of flaunting Fugger's wealth. Interestingly, the stove in the relief on the *kakelugn* also appears to be a tile stove. The *kakelugn* was most likely made by the B H

Lundgrens kakelfabrik around 1900. However, other firms made similar stoves—A Th Sandbäcks kakelfabrik in Kalmar manufactured them circa 1889 and Kakelfabriks AB in Karlskrona made stoves similar to the one in the library around 1900.

The First Chamber/Den/Reading Room

Next to the Library is a small Den or Reading Room. The Den is filled with books and bound periodicals in floor-to-ceiling bookcases. The bookcases may originally have been in the office of the *Svenska Amerikanska Posten* in downtown Minneapolis. In one corner of the room is a well-worn leather chair that Swan Turnblad used. A photograph from the 1930s shows a pair of the chairs in the den and two leather rocking chairs in the Library. The photograph, taken looking from the Library into the Den, shows heavy drapes hanging in the doorways and tied back to the doorframes. The olive green drapes have a design woven into the top and bottom borders and also the Swedish national coat of arms and the year. The drapes are currently in storage.

The *kakelugn* in the Den, white with pastel and gold trim, has moldings of fanciful birds on the front. It was made by *Uppsala-Ekeby AB* in Uppsala, Sweden. A small room, originally a bathroom, links the den with the Second Chamber, now the Glass Room.

The Second Chamber/Glass Room

The Second Chamber contains a *kakelugn* in the Rococo Revival style, made in Uppsala, Sweden, by *Uppsala-Ekeby AB*. Colors of the tile stove are

The kakelugn in the Glass Room has an elaborately scalloped top.

Kakelugnen i glasrummet har ett snäckskalsinspirerat krön.

The large rooms on the second floor are arranged around the balcony. Changes have been made to this area since this photo was taken.

De stora rummen på andra våningen är samlade runt balkongen.

echoed in the polychromed ceiling, which was restored by Marvin A. Anderson and Curt Pederson in the mid-1980s.

Originally the room was probably a bedroom for Swan Turnblad, but for many years it has been used to display the American Swedish Institute's collection of traditional and contemporary Swedish glass. Many of the glassmaking firms are located in the province of Småland in southern Sweden, where Swan Turnblad was born.

The Third Chamber

This room, linking two of the largest rooms, which were possibly bedrooms for the Turnblads, may have served as a dressing room or a small sitting room for the Turnblads. Note the two mahogany doors, each with full-length mirrors and set at angles that would give viewers a complete view of the clothing they wore. Behind one door is a closet; the other door opens to a full bathroom. There is also a tile stove, with a delicate shell design, in this room. Currently, the room is used for exhibits.

The third chamber, connecting the Glass and the Blue Rooms, was probably originally a dressing room. Handsome mirrored doors set at angles opposite each other lead to a bathroom and a closet.

Tredje kammaren, mellan det blå rummet och glasrummet, var antagligen från början ett omklädningsrum. Vackra spegelförsedda dörrar satta i vinkel mittemot varandra leder till ett badrum och en garderob.

The Fourth Chamber/Blue Room

The fourth chamber, known also as the Blue Room because of the beautiful baby blue color of the *kakelugn,* is spacious and may have been used as a sitting room or bedroom by Mrs. Turnblad. The Blue Room is directly above the Dining Room on the first floor and it has the same floor plan. At one end is a bow window that reaches almost from the floor to the ceiling, letting in much light. On either side of the stove, which is set in a recessed alcove, are carved wooden benches.

The baby blue kakelugn is what gives the Blue Room its currently used name.

Den ljusblå kakelugnen har givit blå rummet dess nuvarande namn.

The Blue Room is now used as a gallery for temporary exhibits, both from the ASI collection and from other sources.

The Fifth Chamber/ Lillian Turnblad Room

The fifth chamber, connected to the Blue Room, was probably the bedroom of Lillian Turnblad. The room contains a *kakelugn* in the Rococo Revival style with a white background. It is decorated in pastel tones of green, pink and yellow. Colors on the polychromed ceiling, which was painted by Marvin A. Anderson and Curt Pederson in 1988, reflect those of the *kakelugn*. A bathroom and closet originally connected to the chamber. Early photographs of the room show portieres (drapes) in the doorway leading into the Blue Room, as in the other rooms on the second floor.

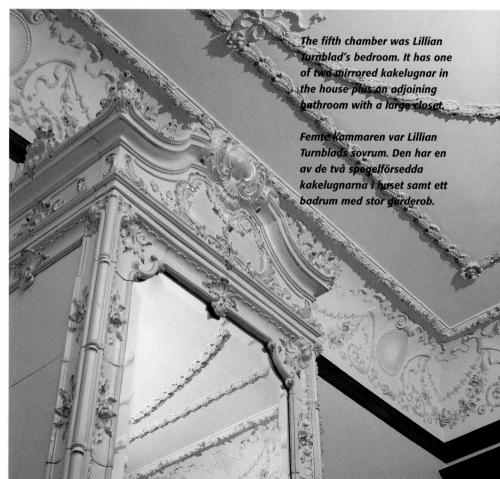

The fifth chamber was Lillian Turnblad's bedroom. It has one of two mirrored kakelugnar in the house plus an adjoining bathroom with a large closet.

Femte kammaren var Lillian Turnblads sovrum. Den har en av de två spegelförsedda kakelugnarna i huset samt ett badrum med stor garderob.

"A wonderful place for playing hide-and-seek"

Elinor Hansen Strot, daughter of caretaker Ben Hansen, wore a confirmation gown made by her mother from organdy curtains that once hung in the carriage house.

Elinor Hansen Strot, dotter till vaktmästaren Ben Hansen, i en konfirmationsklänning som hennes mor hade sytt av organdigardiner som en gång hängt i annexet.

The four Hansen children, whose father, Ben Hansen, was the caretaker and chauffeur for the Turnblads, had a real-life castle for a playhouse. The Hansens, Norwegian immigrants, moved into the caretaker's apartment in the upper floor of the carriage house shortly after Ben Hansen was hired to work for Swan Turnblad in 1933. Hansen's oldest daughter, Elinor Hansen Strot, recalled that Turnblad nearly didn't hire her dad because he was a Norwegian. "But my mother was half-Swedish," Ben Hansen said to Turnblad. "Well, I'll try you out then," said Turnblad, and hired him.

After a short time, Turnblad asked Hansen if he and his family would move into the caretaker's apartment so they could keep an eye on the empty house. However, Turnblad said he wanted to meet the children before he let them move in. So the three little Hansen girls—ten-year-old Elinor and her younger sisters Ada and Gretta—dressed in their fanciest lace-collared Sunday best frocks, with bows in their hair and white gloves on their hands, met Swan Turnblad.

Elinor remembers little about what was actually said at the meeting, but added, "He was a very austere man. We had to curtsy to him and he asked us our names and just said a few things to us." Turnblad must have thought the family suitable, as he gave permission for them to live in the caretaker's quarters. Later that spring, Turnblad died. A few hours after his death, on May 17, 1933, the fourth Hansen child, Henry, was born. "Miss [Lillian] Turnblad always thought that was special, that Henry was born so close to the time of her father's death."

"For years, on the anniversary of her father's death and Henry's birthday, she visited her father's grave and later she would bring Henry one rose for every year of his life. Of course, Henry would much rather have had a toy," said Strot.

The Hansen children helped their parents with the caretaking chores in the big house, dusting the seemingly endless miles of carved woodwork. However, they also had time to play. Henry admits that he used to slide down the banister of the beautiful staircase that leads up from the mansion's Grand Hall. He also scrambled in and out of the carriage house doors through the flap meant as a door for pets. The children played hide-and-seek in the big house. "It was quite a good place for hide-and-seek," said Strot. "We used to hide between the pairs of drapes that were hung in the doorways of the rooms on the second floor. Closets and cupboards were good hiding places, too. My friends loved to come over. They would say, 'Oh, you live in the castle.' The house was kind of spooky, though. You had the feeling someone could be lurking there."

Lillian Turnblad took an interest in the children, often telling Ben Hansen to bring the girls to the Academy of the Holy Angels, where she lived after her father's death, so that they could see the plays that the students put on. Afterwards, Miss Turnblad treated the girls to hot chocolate and cookies. When Lillian Turnblad found out that Elinor liked to read, she gave her the key to the library of the house at 2600 Park Avenue. Elinor spent hours curled up in a big black leather chair reading Lillian Turnblad's books. "I would just lose myself in the books—all the Louisa May Alcott books—I enjoyed them so much. Sometimes my mother would have to call me to come back home."

The "castle's" nooks and crannies made wonderful hiding places for the Hansen children as well as this little boy.

"Slottets" vinklar och vrår var underbara gömställen för såväl Hansens barn som denne lille pojke.

The Third Floor

The third floor of the Turnblad mansion is dominated by the large Ballroom, which is surrounded by smaller rooms, used by guests and by the servants. Some of the rooms are not open to the public; others contain exhibits from the ASI collection.

The Ballroom and Lobby

The spacious Ballroom has a proscenium stage, where an orchestra would have played for dances, if any had been held. In the center of the ceiling of the Ballroom is a frosted glass skylight. The Ballroom was probably used for a 1921 celebration of the Aero Club. The club was formed in 1917 to recruit pilots for World War I; members of the club included many of the Twin Cities' most prominent families.

In 1996, a permanent exhibit on Swedish-American life in Minneapolis and St. Paul was installed in the Ballroom.

The spacious third-floor Ballroom has a skylight and a stage. The other third-floor rooms are arranged around it.

Den rymliga balsalen på tredje våningen har takfönster och en scen. De övriga rummen på denna våning ligger runt om den.

Double doors from the Ballroom lead into a lobby, where built-in benches would have afforded Ballroom guests a chance to rest. On one side of the lobby are small servants' rooms, which are closed to the public and used for storage. On the lobby's other side is a large bathroom with a skylight and a large bathtub directly beneath it; this is not open to the public. Two guest bedrooms are next to the full bathroom, with a half bath—also not open—between the second bedroom and a third bedroom. The third bedroom now has a weaving exhibit.

The Weaving Room

Originally a guest bedroom, the Weaving Room has windows on two sides and drawers built into the wall. It is used for exhibits, currently one on the life and work of Hilma Berglund, the Swedish-American woman who was a pioneer in weaving education at the University of Minnesota. Examples from the ASI collection of Berglund's textiles and other works are displayed in the room.

The Studio

On the other side of the Ballroom is the Studio, which has a large skylight. It was used as a working art studio for Lillian Turnblad, who reportedly liked to paint by natural light. She enjoyed painting and took art lessons. The Studio has built-in cabinets for storing brushes and other art supplies. One of her paintings, of two young girls chatting with a man who appears to be a hiker, hangs in an alcove in this room. The Studio is also used for display of items from the ASI collection.

Many Swedish immigrants brought weaving skills with them. The Weaving Room contains looms and examples of weaving.

Många svenska immigranter var duktiga på att väva. Vävkammaren med vävstolar och vävnader.

Lillian Turnblad was an amateur painter who may have used the studio to create some of her paintings. The studio has a skylight and views of downtown Minneapolis.

Lillian Turnblad var amatörmålare och kan ha använt ateljén då hon målade en del av sina tavlor. Ateljén har takfönster och utsikt över centrala Minneapolis.

The lower level has been altered since this photo was taken, but the kakelugn—with its Viking motifs and tomtar—remains as it was.

Bottenvåningen har förändrats sedan detta foto togs, men kakelugnen med sina vikinga-motiv och tomtar är densamma.

The Lower Level

The lower level of the mansion has changed very much from how it appears in the heating blue-prints. Then, plans for the lower level included a billiard room, smoking room, vegetable storage room, wine cellar, laundry, gymnasium and swimming pool. There is no evidence that the gymnasium and the pool were ever built. Much of the other space in the lower level has been altered over the years as ASI needs for serving its members and visitors changed.

The Lounge and Adjacent Rooms

The wide staircase leads down from the Grand Hall and opens into a large room that was formerly used as an assembly room. One of the mansion's most unusual *kakelugnar* is in this room. It is dec-orated with Viking motifs, with a likeness of the Norse god Thor in the center. Atop the stove and in niches on either side of the stove's front are mischievous-looking figures that resemble *tomtar,* characters in Swedish folklore. The space is now a

Workmen rest outside the main entrance of the Turnblad house during construction.

Arbetare tar rast utanför huvud-ingången till huset under byggandet.

Master Craftsmen Steiner, Schlink and Polasek

Turnblad's mansion was the work of many craftsmen and laborers over a period of several years. Most of their names are now unknown, but three—stonecarver Herman G. Schlink and woodcarvers Ulrich Steiner and Albin Polasek—stand out, both for their own achievements and for what skill and grace they brought to the Turnblad mansion.

Steiner, born in Switzerland in 1879, was also the son of a woodcarver and he served his apprenticeship in his home town. He immigrated to the United States in 1902 and worked in Wisconsin and California before coming to Minnesota, where he worked for the Aaron Carlson Company, which had the contract for the woodcarving in the Turnblad mansion.

Steiner was one of 18 carvers hired to work on the mansion and he was young, only 26 years old. Several accounts say that he was paid more than the others, although the amounts given vary according to the source. If the others were paid 30 cents an hour, as one account says, Steiner was paid 40 cents an hour. Many of the carvings in the mansion, including the 52 cherubs in the Music Room and the Della Robbia-style wreath over the fireplace in the Dining Room, are Steiner's works. After he completed the work on the mansion, Steiner continued as a woodcarver, working nearly until the time of his death in 1977.

Schlink, born in Winona, Minnesota, in 1869, came to Minneapolis as a young man. He studied at the Art Institute of Chicago before returning to Minnesota. Schlink did the exterior stone carving on the mansion and also designed and either executed or supervised the interior plaster decorations in the house. He continued to work in Minneapolis until he died in 1950.

Albin Polasek, who designed and carved the two-story fireplace mantel in the mansion's Grand Hall and the "barbarians," as he called them, on either side of the fireplace, was born in what is now the Czech Republic in 1879. He immigrated to the United States as a young man and worked as a woodcarver in Wisconsin, where he met and worked with Ulrich Steiner. Polasek was pleased to see Steiner again when he came to Minneapolis to carve the fireplace mantel in the summer of 1906. Polasek later studied at the Pennsylvania Academy of Fine Art and the American Academy in Rome and won many international awards during his career. A museum in Florida is devoted to his work. He died in 1965.

Woodcarvers Ulrich Steiner and Albin Polasek were friends who were pleased to work together on the Turnblad mansion. They are shown here at Minnehaha Falls in Minneapolis.

Träsnidarna Ulrich Steiner och Albin Polasek var vänner som var glada över att få arbeta tillsammans på Turnblads residens. Här är de vid Minnehaha Falls i Minneapolis.

Master stonecarver Herman G. Schlink did the ornamental carving on the exterior of the house and the carriage house, including a freehand carving of a horse's head above the carriage house door.

Mästerstenhuggaren Herman G. Schlink gjorde alla utsmyckningar på exteriören av huset och vagnslidret, inklusive det på fri hand huggna hästhuvudet ovanför dörren.

65

The deep-green kakelugn is in what is now called the Viking room on the lower level.

Den mörkgröna kakelugnen är i det som nu kallas vikingarummet på bottenvåningen.

lounge for visitors, with access to the Viking Room, *Bokhandel* (bookstore), *Kaffestuga* (coffee shop), kitchen, and a women's restroom with an original porcelain sink. Down a hallway are more restrooms and an entrance to the auditorium, as well as stairs and elevator to the ASI business office and archives, located in the carriage house.

The former smoking room, now called the Viking Room, has a beautiful, deep-green tile stove. It is open to the public except when in use for meetings and special events. What was designated as the billiard room is now the *Bokhandel* (bookstore). At the far end of the assembly room is a ramp leading up to the snug *Kaffestuga,* where visitors can obtain refreshments.

The Auditorium

The Auditorium, in which most ASI programs are held, is a relatively recent addition to the Turnblad mansion. It was built in 1983, under the leadership of ASI members who thought more space was needed for programs and celebrations. A serving window from the kitchen enables food to be served easily.

The walls of the Auditorium are adorned with a painted mural that tells both the story of Swedish immigration to America, and particularly to Minnesota, and also records Swedish traditions that have been handed down by Swedish-Americans. Done in the distinctive style of folk painting called *Dalmålning,* after the province of Dalarna, where it is common, the mural was painted by Swedish artist Bengt Engman (1925-1987).

A lively, colorful mural in the Dalarna folk painting tradition adorns the walls of the Auditorium.

En livfull och färgrik dalmålning av Bengt Engman pryder väggarna i auditoriet.

The Auditorium, where many programs are held, is a 1983 addition to the American Swedish Institute.

I auditoriet, en till byggnad från 1983, hålls många program.

The Carriage House/Stable

Originally, according to the heating blueprints made before the mansion and carriage house were actually built, the carriage house was also designated as a stable. There were to be stalls for horses and also a loose box for exercise and, in addition, a cow stall and a manure pit. On the second floor, a hayloft was to be above the stable and a caretaker's apartment occupied the rest of the upper space.

The horse and cow stalls were never constructed, however. By the time the carriage house was built there was no need for horses, as Swan Turnblad was one of the first people in Minneapolis to own and operate an automobile. The car, and subse- quent cars, were stored in the carriage house. They were driven into the building onto a turntable, which was turned around when Turnblad wanted to drive out of the carriage house, thus enabling the car to easily turn around without backing up the long driveway.

The carriage house is now used for office space and for the ASI library and archives. The archives and library, on the second floor, are open during weekday museum hours and can be visited.

The carriage house and the mansion are now con- nected by a link that includes side doors that lead to an elevator and stairs adjacent to the auditorium.

How much did the house cost?

Visitors to the American Swedish Institute often ask how much the house cost to build. Unfortunately, we can give no exact figure. When it and the newspaper and its building were donated by Turnblad in 1929, many local newspapers estimated that the house and the *Posten* building together were worth $1.5 million. By contrast, Minnesota Historical Society records of the house built by railroad magnate James J. Hill in St. Paul in the late 19th century show total costs of $931,275. The Hill house has 42 rooms.

Research carried out by ASI member Lawrence Hammerstrom shows the cost of various aspects of the Turnblad house. The six lots on which the house was built cost Turnblad $10,000 in 1903, according to Hammerstrom. Swan Turnblad obtained a building permit allowing for the masonry construction of the $2^{1}/_{2}$ story stone dwelling and barn (carriage house) for $50,000. The building permit for 650 incandescent lamps and the permit for gas piping for 500 gas lights estimated costs of $2,500 and $2,000 respectively. The gas fixtures have since been capped. Hammerstrom lists many other expenses involving the house in his article titled "How Much Did the Turnblad Mansion Cost?"

The lawsuits brought against Turnblad by disgruntled stockholders of *Svenska Amerikanska Posten* coincided with the time the house was being completed in 1908. Turnblad, in fact, wrote his brother Magnus at one point that he was afraid he would lose everything. Public records show that several of the firms involved in the construction filed liens on the property at 2600 Park Avenue during the early years of construction because they hadn't been paid for work they had done. The liens were later resolved.

Svensk sammanfattning/Swedish Summary

Turnblad och hans slott

År 1929, alldeles innan börsmarknaden kraschade och den stora depressionen började, var Minneapolis fortfarande i stort sett en immigranternas stad. De svenskar, norrmän, tyskar, irländare och andra som bodde där talade sitt modersmål och många svenska och norska lutherska kyrkor hade gudstjänster på det gamla landets språk.

En del av dem som bosatte sig i det nya landet hade stor framgång i livet och blev därför betraktade med både beundran och avund. En av dessa var Swan J. Turnblad, en fattig pojke från ett av Sveriges fattigaste landskap. Han gjorde sig stora pengar på en svenskspråkig tidning, gjorde nästan konkurs, kom på fötter igen och lämnade till sist detta kulturarv på Park Avenue 2600.

Det här är berättelsen om Turnblad och huset han byggde, numera American Swedish Institute.

Några månader efter det att hans fru Christina hade dött i september 1929 flyttade Turnblad med sin dotter Lillian till en lägenhet på femte våningen i sydvästra hörnet av en nybyggd fastighet på Park Avenue 2615, mitt emot sitt "palats". Där satt han ofta i fönstret och såg hur folk gick ut och in i hans forna hem, som idag ofta kallas "slottet".

Hur var han egentligen—denne svenske immigrant? Det är väldigt svårt att beskriva honom för Turnblad var, som de flesta, en motsägelsernas man. Han kunde vara snäll och sentimental, sträng och fordrande. Ibland var han mycket generös, andra gånger räknade han varje öre. En del säger att han och hans familj var enstöringar men uppgifter om att han var närvarande vid många privata och kommunala evenemang motsäger detta.

Swan Turnblads liv i Sverige

Swan Turnblad var född den 7 oktober 1860 på en bondgård i Tubbemåla, Vislanda socken, Kronobergs län. Hans föräldrar, Ingjerd Månsdotter och Olof Månsson, döpte honom till Sven Johan samma dag han föddes. När familjen emigrerade till USA blev efternamnet ändrat till Turnblad. Sven Johan Olofsson fick namnet Swan J. Turnblad.

En av Johans halvbröder, Peter Olofsson, var född 1839. Han var alltså 21 år gammal när Sven Johan föddes. Peter Olofsson lämnade Sverige 1864 och bosatte sig i Vasa, Minnesota, och det var också dit resten av familjen senare flyttade.

När Sven Johan var sex år gammal lämnade familjen Tubbemåla och bosatte sig på Södregård,

Långhult. Sedan flyttade de till Norregård, Ryssby socken, Kronobergs län. Man vet inte exakt varför de emigrerade till Amerika.

Mellan åren 1863 och 1877 emigrerade nästan 135.000 svenskar till USA, 40 procent under 1868 och 1869. Allt som allt lämnade ungefär 1.250.000 svenskar sitt hemland från 1845 till 1930. Det var mellan 20 och 25 procent av befolkningen.

Amerika lockar

Hungersnöden i Sverige och erbjudandet om land i Amerika var två av orsakerna till att så många svenskar emigrerade.

Så kallade amerikabrev, skrivna av svenska immigranter, förekom i lokaltidningar i Sverige och lockade många att emigrera. Minnesota Board of Immigration gav till och med ut en broschyr på svenska som höjde livet i Minnesota till skyarna.

Resan till Amerika

Olof Månsson och hans familj lämnade Sverige 1868, och liksom många emigranter reste de först till Liverpool, England, där de gick ombord på SS City of New York. Efter cirka nio dagar till sjöss kom de till New York den 25 september 1868.

Som de flesta svenska emigranter tog familjen båt till Hull, England, tåg till Liverpool och atlantångare till New York. En enkel biljett mellan Göteborg och Chikago, Illinois, kostade ungefär 41 dollar.

Den lilla staden på prärien

Efter att ha gått igenom alla immigrationsformaliteter vid Castle Garden fortsatte resan, troligtvis med tåg, till Red Wing via Chikago. Resans mål, Vasa, är ett litet samhälle på prärien i sydöstra Minnesota inte långt från Red Wing och Mississippifloden. Hans Mattson, som senare blev Minnesotas departementschef och Eric Norelius, en ledare inom Augustana Lutheran Synod, var redan bosatta i Vasa.

Man vet inte mycket om Turnblads uppväxttid i Vasa annat än att han konfirmerades i Vasas Swedish Lutheran Church i maj 1876. Man tror också att han för hand tryckte en lärobok i matematik åt sin lärare P.T. Lindholm år 1877.

Swan och Christina Turnblad

År 1880 bodde Swan Turnblad på Cedar Avenue 127 tillsammans med sin syster och svåger, Mary och Charles Fridlund. Enligt uppgift arbetade han som sättare på *Minnesota Stats Tidning* och bodde på samma adress åren 1881-1883.

Ungefär vid den här tiden flyttade Christina Nilsson till Minneapolis. Hon gifte sig senare med Swan Turnblad. Christina, Kerstin, föddes och döptes i Tångeråsen, Offerdal socken, i Jämtland. Hennes föräldrar hette Gabriel Nilsson och Brita Göransdotter. När hon var 14 år gammal, år 1875, emigrerade hennes far och brodern Göran till USA och bosatte sig nära Slayton, Murray County, i södra Minnesota. Christina och hennes bror Simon kom dit 1876. Och följande år, i maj 1877, var också deras mor och systern Brita i Slayton. Christina konfirmerades i en kyrka i Murray County år 1878.

När hon fyllde 18 år i februari 1879 började Christina arbeta som "dining room girl", servitris, på ett hotell i Worthington. Hon fick $153.53 för ett års arbete.

Christinas bror Göran dog i tuberkulos 1879 och hennes mor dog i samma sjukdom 1881. Christina flyttade troligtvis till Minneapolis före år 1882. Man vet att hon arbetade i Carlsons Bokhandel och bodde på 2nd Street 1204 åren 1882-1883. Hon och Swan Turnblad träffades på ett godtemplarmöte eller dans och gifte sig den 28 april 1883 i Augustana Lutheran Church i Minneapolis bara två månader innan hennes far dog. Därefter bodde Brita hos sin syster och svåger.

Christinas bror Simon Nilsson dog i tuberkulos i maj 1884. Han var gift och hade en dotter, Anna Severine, bara en månad gammal. Följande år dog Brita Nilsson, Christinas syster, också hon i tuberkulos. När Simons änka dog blev Swan Turnblad förmyndare för Anna Severine, Christinas brorsdotter.

Den enda ljuspunkten i allt detta var att Turnblads enda barn, dottern Lillian Zenobia, föddes den 2 september 1884. Hon döptes några veckor senare i Augustana Lutheran Church. Lillian, som var artistisk och musikalisk, gick i tre olika skolor, först Northwestern Conservatory of Music, sedan St.

Joseph's Academy i St. Paul och till slut Convent of the Sacred Heart i Montréal, Kanada där hon tog sin examen.

Turnblads roll i samhället

Under årens lopp tillhörde Swan Turnblad många organisationer och var mycket aktiv i kommunala sammanhang. Ett av hans och Christinas största intressen var dock nykterhetsrörelsen. De var trogna medlemmar av Freya Society, en nykterhetsorganisation.

Turnblad kunde skämta ibland. På en middag för att hedra Dr. V. Hugo Wickström, redaktör på Jämtlands Posten, serverades bland annat pressoppa, journalistfrikadeller, rapportörfrukt och tryckfrihetsoliver.

Turnblad kom nog också ihåg hur det var att vara hungrig i Sverige. År 1902 ledde han en kampanj för att samla in $20.000 till de människor som svalt i norra Sverige. För sitt bistånd fick han år 1926 Nordstjärneorden, som nu finns på American Swedish Institute.

Turnblad blev amerikansk medborgare 1895. Han var sekreterare i North Star Republican Club 1896 men 1904 och 1908 var han delegat vid det demokratiska partiets konvent.

Swan Turnblads privata liv och resor

Turnblads älskade att resa och Swan Turnblads

personliga reseskildringar blev mycket uppskattade av *Svenska Amerikanska Postens* läsare. Trots att hans fru och dotter var med på hans resor nämnde han dem nästan aldrig.

I juni 1895 reste familjen för första gången till Sverige och Norge. Två år senare var det övriga Europas tur: England, Frankrike, Belgien, Tyskland, Danmark och Sverige.

Så här skriver Turnblad i *Posten* den 6/7 1897 under rubriken "Gamla kära minnen":

> "Gårdagen var en dag, som jag länge kommer att bevara i mitt minne. Jag hade då nöjet besöka den plats och den stuga, der min vagga stått, nemligen Norregård i Tubbamåla.

> I Söregård bodde Samuel Magnusson, som kände väl till hela vår familj. Af honom inbjödos vi på kaffe och voffler. Här, märkligt nog, sammanträffade jag med hans syster, Elin Magnusson, som var min gudmor. Tårarne stodo henne i ögonen, när hon började omtala gamla minnen och erinrade sig vänner, som för närvarande äro bosatta i St. Peter, Minnesota. Hon omtalade också sin forna lekkamrat, moster Turnquist i Vasa.

> Efter ett besök i dessa nejder, undrar jag visst icke uppå, att så många smålänningar resa till Amerika, och att de der kunna svinga sig upp i likhet med en Hon. John Lind (Lind var guvernör i Minnesota)...ty det är visst och säkert, att det är deras medfödda, i hemlandet insupna fasta karaktär och företagsamhet, och icke några penningearf från barndomshemmen, som varit orsaken till deras uppkomst i verlden."

Under besöket i Sverige stannade Turnblad till i Göteborg där han köpte J.B. Gans bibliotek—6.000 band—som han sedan lät *Svenska Amerikanska Postens* prenumeranter låna. En del av dessa böcker finns nu i arkivet och biblioteket på ASI.

År 1899 var Turnblads återigen i Europa—den här gången Belgien, Nederländerna, Tyskland, Danmark, Sverige, Schweiz, Italien och Frankrike. Enligt en artikel i *Minneapolis Journal* var det möjligt för Turnblad att närvara vid den beryktade Dreyfusrättegången. Som bekant hade Alfred Dreyfus, en fransk arméofficer, blivit orättfärdigt dömd för högförräderi och fallet måste omprövas.

I april 1902 tillbringade Turnblads flera veckor i Italien, Grekland, Turkiet, Ryssland, Finland och Sverige.

I Posten den 24/6 1902 kunde man läsa följande:

> "Jag hade väntat mig finna grekerna lika otrefliga som italienarne om ej ännu mera men blef härvid ganska behagligt öfverraskad. Efter att öfver tre veckors tid ha vistats bland de något stormiga italienarne, hvilka vid hvarje tillfälle söka att pungslå turisterna, synes det ganska behagligt att komma bland ett folk, som är ovanligt hyfsadt, tillmötesgående och ordentligt. Grekerna (åtminstone de vi kommit i beröring med här i Athen) äro mycket liknande den svenska befolkningen. I alla land som jag förut besökt har jag aldrig sett något folk som så mycket liknar det svenska som just grekerna."

En mycket modern man

I mångt och mycket var Turnblad före sin tid. Han köpte den allra modernaste maskinutrustningen för tidningens räkning. Och i Minneapolis var han den förste som hade bil. Det var en Waverley Electric, tillverkad i Indianapolis, Indiana, 1899. Den kostade $1.250 plus frakt.

Enligt Robert R. Johnson var Turnblads Waverley den första kommersiellt tillverkade bilen i Minneapolis. Bilar kallades på den tiden "horseless carriages", hästlösa vagnar. Den 10 april 1900 stod det i *Minneapolis Journal:*

> "Man kunde igår kväll se den första privatägda bilen i staden. Den tillhör Swan J. Turnblad som äger Svenska Amerikanska Posten. Det blev stor uppståndelse när Turnblad och några vänner kom åkande längs Nicollet Avenue. Fordonet är av senaste modell och har alla moderna finesser. Man kan köra fem till sju svenska mil på en laddning i fem olika hastigheter. Herr Turnblad har installerat en liten elektrisk generator i sitt vagnslider så att han kan ladda upp batteriet när det behövs."

Turnblads andra bil var en Knox Waterless, 1903 års modell, och hans tredje bil, år 1908, en Winton Touring car. Den hade sex cylindrar och 48 hästkrafter och kostade $4.500. Hans fjärde bil, år 1910, var en Columbus Electric med plats för fyra passagerare. Det var inte en cabriolet och den var registrerad i Christina Turnblads namn.

Turnblads mest spännande bilresa var utan tvivel den av American Automobile Club anordnade resan till världsutställningen i St. Louis år 1904. Trots många problem med bilen, bland annat motorstopp och bromsar som inte fungerade, skrev Turnblad entusiastiskt om resan i *Minneapolis Journal* den 13/8 1904: "Resan från vår blåsiga

stad Minneapolis via Chikago till St. Louis var en av de trevligaste jag har gjort." Folk på landsbygden stod utefter vägen, hurrade, vinkade och kastade frukt och blommor till bilförare och passagerare. Både Christina och Lillian var med på resan.

Christina och Lillian Turnblads tillbakadragna liv

Mycket har skrivits om Swan Turnblad men man vet inte mycket om hans hemliv tillsammans med Christina och Lillian. Några få julklappar, bland annat en liten porslinshund från Rörstrand med Christinas och Lillians namn målade på tassarna, finns i institutets samlingar.

Detta är Christinas dödsannons i *Svenska Amerikanska Posten* år 1929:

> "Mrs. Christina N. Turnblad, 68 år gammal, hustru till Swan J. Turnblad, utgivare och chef för Svenska Amerikanska Posten, avled stilla och fridfullt fredagen den 6 september efter ett tåligt buret långt lidande på St. Barnabas sjukhus. Begravningen ägde rum i Lakewood Cemeterys begravningskapell den 9 september."

Lillian Turnblad var redaktör på *Posten* från sin fars död tills den såldes år 1940.

Redan som ung var hon intresserad av konst, tog lektioner i målning och målade själv. I museet finns en av hennes tavlor och en möbelgrupp i dalablått med blommor som hon lär ha målat. Lillian var en kraftig kvinna, anspråkslöst klädd på de fotografier som finns bevarade. Men det finns ett undantag, ett mycket vackert fotografi i färg av Lillian i trettioårsåldern där hon har en dräkt från Värend på sig och småler mot fotografen.

Efter faderns död flyttade Lillian till Academy of Holy Angels i Richfield, då rena rama landet men nu en förort till Minneapolis. Hon blev aldrig katolik men kände sig som hemma hos nunnorna. Enligt syster Hubert Marie som kom till Academy of Holy Angels 1931 var Lillian vän till syster Caritas som hade hand om undervisningen i konst på Academy of Holy Angels. Hon hade sitt eget bord i matsalen, åt ensam på sitt eget vackra porslin, hämtades varje morgon och kördes till arbetet i en limousine.

Ett brev skrivet år 1937 av syster Marie Teresa säger detta om Lillian: "Jag kände henne som flicka när jag var lärare på St. Agatha's Conservatory och vi blev genast goda vänner. Hon bad mig måla ett porträtt som hon själv satt modell för och nu har jag blivit ombedd att måla både hennes mors och hennes fars porträtt men de måste skissas och målas med fotografier som förebild." Porträtten hänger nu på American Swedish Institute.

Lillian Turnblad dog i oktober 1943, 59 år gammal. Hon lämnade nettoavkastningen från sin förmögenhet till Hennepin Countys avdelning av det amerikanska Röda korset så länge krig pågick och därefter i ett år efter det att fred hade tillkännagivits av USAs president. Efter krigsslutet skulle fonden gå till Minneapolis Institute of Arts. Hon lämnade inga pengar till American Swedish Institute, vilket många hade väntat sig att hon skulle göra. När hon dog värderades hennes förmögenhet till nästan $300.000. Christina N. och Swan J. Turnblads minnesfond skulle, enligt Lillians testamente, användas för inköp av konstverk av högsta klass och kvalitet till konstmuseets permanenta samlingar och värdet är idag mellan en och två millioner dollar.

Den 3 november 1943 överklagades testamentet av hennes två kusiner, men domstolens utslag den 2 december 1943 bekräftade att testamentet ägde laga kraft.

Inte vilken immigranttidning som helst

De flesta av de cirka 350 svenskspråkiga tidningar som utgavs blev inte långlivade. År 1880 fanns det 16 svenskspråkiga tidningar som gavs ut en gång i veckan. Tio år senare hade antalet ökat till 41. *Svenska Amerikanska Posten* kom ut för första gången år 1885 och utgavs sedan i 55 år. Den överlevde fyra andra svenskspråkiga tidningar i Minnesota.

Enligt Chikagojournalisten C.F. Peterson var Turnblad "mer amerikansk än svensk, det vill säga djärvare och mer energisk när det gällde affärer, lugnare och mer beräknande...vilket gjorde att han hade stor framgång som affärsman." Han anlitade både lokala och nationella reklambyråer, fick fler och fler prenumeranter och annonsörer och lät läsarna veta hur framgångsrik *Posten* var. Tidningen hade 10.000 läsare 1887, och 1888 års nyårslöfte var: "Nästa år kommer vi att ha 20.000 prenumeranter."

För att få läsare erbjöd *Posten* sina prenumeranter många premier, bland annat en klocka, "den vackraste i sitt slag som någonsin tillverkats". Prenumeranterna kunde köpa denna klocka för $2.50 trots att den var värd minst $5.

Posten var från början en förespråkare för nykterhetsrörelsen. Men enligt de anteckningar som Magnus Turnblad, Swans bror, lämnade fick denna mindre inflytande när Swan Turnblad blev redaktör. För att utöka läsarantalet skulle nu allt material av vikt behandlas på ett opartiskt sätt. Bara de senaste och bästa nyheterna skulle införas och man skulle rikta sin uppmärksamhet mot den svenska delen. Följetongerna skulle bli mer spännande och mer lärorika än tidigare och man skulle inte glömma dikter, sketcher och noveller. Nykterhetsrörelsens budskap fanns dock med i bilden.

År 1904 hade *Posten* ett nytt utseende. Man använde färg och hade speciella sidor för kvinnor, barn och trädgårdsskötsel; till och med serier förekom.

Turnblad och hans hund Toby var oskiljaktiga vänner. Hilda Benson skriver i sina memoarer: "Toby hade en pingla i halsbandet...så när vi hörde den visste vi att chefen var i antågande. Toby hade ett badkar nere i källaren i Postenfastigheten. Jag kan fortfarande se herr Turnblad med handduken över armen och Toby vid sin sida på väg till badet."

Swan Turnblad sålde *Posten* till Magnus Martinson år 1920 men år 1927 gjorde denne konkurs. Turnblad köpte tillbaka tidningen och förblev dess utgivare med hjälp av Lillian till sin död.

Posten blev mindre och mindre och när den såldes

år 1940 var den en åttasidig tidning med få annonser. I sitt farväl till läsarna onsdagen den 11 september 1940 skrev Lillian följande: "...Att Amerikas svenskstat framför andra—Minnesota—nu mister sitt eget svenska organ är ett beklagligt förhållande, men det är ingenting att göra åt den saken.

Varje tidning har sin egen prägel och Svenska Amerikanska Posten har haft sin. Den betecknas inte endast av tidningens vignett utan av hela dess innehåll. Tidningens ägare och utgivare under ett 40-tal år...Mr. Swan J. Turnblad, bestämde redan från början att tidningen skulle verka för gudsfruktan, nykterhet, och folkuppfostran och den har aldrig svikit detta program. Samtidigt har den sökt att främja svensk kultur här i landet och att vara en god och pålitlig nyhetstidning. Tusentals av våra prenumeranter ha tacksamt erkänt att vi gått den rätta vägen i dessa fall. Personligen kunna vi endast säga att vi gjort vårt bästa och att om brister förelegat de inte berott på att den goda viljan saknats. Till alla våra läsare framföra vi ett hjärtevarmt tack för de år som gått. Det finns prenumeranter som haft denna tidning i många, många år. Och vi veta att de komma att sakna den." *Lillian Turnblad*

De sista åren och grundandet av American Swedish Institute

Redan innan Christina Turnblad dog hösten 1929 hade familjen tydligen bestämt sig för att skänka sitt hem på Park Avenue till svenskkolonin. Turnblad hade redan år 1925 pratat med den svenske konsuln Nils Jaenson om att donera fastigheten till en svensk institution.

Från början insisterade Turnblad på att $100.000 skulle insamlas för att kunna underhålla huset. Jaenson gick inte med på detta och underhandlingarna drog ut på tiden. Till slut bestämde Turnblad sig för att donera fastigheten till en svensk stiftelse. Sveriges kronprins Gustav Adolf accepterade tacksamt donationen per brev den 22 juli 1929 och lovade att bli institutets beskyddare förutsatt att donationen var bindande och att tillräckliga medel fanns för underhåll.

I tidningsintervjuer sade Turnblad att han under en längre tid hade planerat att ge huset till svenskarna. "Många undrade kanske varför en så liten familj som vår...ville ha ett så stort hus. Nu kanske de förstår varför...I hela mitt liv har det varit min ambition att omhulda, befordra, gynna och bevara svensk kultur i Amerika. Mycket av det som är svenskt håller jag kärt fastän jag nu är amerikan...och det tycks mig vara önskvärt för båda länderna att vissa aspekter av svensk kultur visas här."

Swan Turnblad dog den 17 maj 1933 och begravdes bredvid sin hustru Christina på Lakewood Cemetery i Minneapolis.

Huset

Ingen vet när och var Swan Turnblad fick idén till huset. Han kanske var imponerad av de slott han såg i Frankrike och kanske hade han sett stora herr-gårdar i södra Sverige när han var barn. Kanske var det hans dröm om Amerika att bygga ett stort hus på Minneapolis societetsgata framför andra. Många av de mest framgångsrika och välbärgade familjerna bodde på Park Avenue. Turnblad valde två relativt unga arkitekter, Christopher A. Boehme och Victor Cordella, att göra ritningarna. Man började bygga år 1904 och huset var klart för inflyttning år 1908. Huset är utan tvivel ett slott, ofta kallat det svenska slottet. Men svenska besökare tycker kanske att det är ett amerikanskt slott.

Huset har tre våningar om 33 rum plus källare och vind. Det som kanske mest fascinerar svenska besökare är alla fantastiska skapelser i trä och sten: lejon, gripar, delfiner, hästar, keruber och två "barbarer" på var sida om den öppna spisen i den stora entréhallen. Huset har också en imponerande samling kakelugnar, nio av dem tillverkade i Sverige. Taken i stuckatur renoveras allt eftersom medel blir tillgängliga. Under årens lopp har American Swedish Institute välkomnat många välkända besökare, bland andra Sveriges nuvarande kung och drottning, Dwight Eisenhower, Jan Troell, Max von Sydow, Ann Margret och sist men inte minst Astrid Lindgren.

Entréhallen

Här finner man de två "barbarer" som tidigare nämnts. På var sida om klockan kan man se två kvinnofigurer; en representerar dag, den andra natt. Ovanför detta står en viking omgiven av pelare. Allra högst kan man se en byst av en viking. Allt detta är snidat i afrikansk mahogny av Albin Polasek. På var sida om den öppna spisen står två stora porslinsurnor med elefanthuvuden från Rörstrand.

Salongen

Vid sekelskiftet hade alla förmögna hem en salong. Denna är i rokokostil och används för utställningar. Rummet har restaurerats av Gertrude Gump.

Sällskapsrummet

Ett moriskinspirerat rum med en mycket vacker kakelugn tillverkad av Rörstrand. Ett gammalt foto visar att denna kakelugn har använts trots att centralvärme installerades när huset byggdes. Används nu som presentbutik, ASI Museum Shop.

Matsalen

De detaljrikaste sniderierna finner man i matsalen: blommor, frukt och kransar i ek och mahogny från Honduras. Ovanför den öppna spisen i marmor från Kolmården kan man se *Den bergtagna*. Den väggfasta byffén med konkava och konvexa glasdörrar är, liksom allt annat i trä, gjord av Ulrich Steiner.

Frukostrummet

Det här är ett rum med gustavianska möbler från Sverige. Kakelugnen är i nyrokoko och från Rörstrand. Moraklockan är 1700-tal och porträttet är målat av Gustaf Hesselius (1682-1755), den första erkända svenskamerikanska konstnären i USA.

Musikrummet

Här har vi keruber, allt som allt 52, i mahogny från Honduras, alla snidade av Ulrich Steiner. Rummet restaurerades av Marvin A. Anderson och Curt Pederson 1980-1981.

Visbyfönstret

Det här är en kopia av Carl Gustaf Hellqvists målning *Valdemar Atterdag brandskattar Visby* som finns på Nationalmuseum i Stockholm. Fönstret tillverkades av Neuman och Vogel i Stockholm år 1908.

Andra våningen
Biblioteket

Här finns Swan J. Turnblads böcker i ett rum med paneler av blekt amerikansk valnöt. Kakelugnen skildrar kejsar Karl V:s besök hos Jacob Fugger, en av Europas mest välbärgade köpmän, i Augsburg omkring år 1520.

Första kammaren/Läsrummet

Bokhyllor från golv till tak som troligtvis kom från *Svenska Amerikanska Posten*. En gammal nött läderfåtölj som var Turnblads favoritstol. Kakelugnen med fåglar är tillverkad av Uppsala Ekeby Kakelugnsfabrik.

Andra kammaren/Glasrummet

Från början var detta antagligen Swan Turnblads sovrum. Nu används det för att visa institutets imponerande samling av gammalt och nytt glas.

Tredje kammaren

Det här var ett omklädningsrum eller möjligtvis ett litet vardagsrum mellan de två största kamrarna. Bakom två spegelförsedda dörrar finns ett badrum och en garderob.

Fjärde kammaren/Blå rummet

Den vackra blå kakelugnen som står i en alkov omgiven av snidade träbänkar har givit namn till detta rum. Det var troligtvis fru Turnblads vardagsrum eller sovrum. Nu används det som utställningslokal för temporära utställningar.

Femte kammaren/Lillian Turnblads rum

Det här är ett relativt litet rum med en kakelugn i nyrokoko med vit bakgrund och pastellfärger i grönt, rosa och gult. Då taket restaurerades 1988 användes samma färgsättning.

Tredje våningen

Den här våningen i residenset domineras av en stor balsal omgiven av rum för gäster och anställda. Dubbeldörrar leder till en foajé med väggfasta bänkar där gästerna kunde vila sig mellan danserna. Man vet dock inte om Turnblads hade många gäster, för endast en tillställning finns dokumenterad. Det var Aero Club, en organisation som hade bildats 1917 för att rekrytera piloter till första världskriget, som hade ett samkväm. Många av dess medlemmar tillhörde Minneapolis och St. Pauls mest prominenta familjer, som nu inbjöds till residenset.

År 1996 installerades i balsalen en permanent utställning om svenskt liv i Minneapolis och St. Paul. Några av rummen häruppe används till förvaring av institutets samlingar och är inte öppna för allmänheten.

Vävkammaren

Ett före detta gästrum som används som utställningslokal för ASIs textilsamlingar. För närvarande finner man här Hilma Berglunds livsverk. Hon var pionjär inom vävkonsten, svenskamerikanska och textillärare på University of Minnesota.

Studion

Lillian Turnblad var lyckligt lottad. Hon hade en studio med allt vad det innebär: takfönster, gott om utrymme och inbyggda skåp för penslar, färg och dylikt.

Bottenvåningen

Bottenvåningen ser helt annorlunda ut nu än den gjorde på arkitekternas ritningar. Två kakelugnar finns kvar. Den som står nära foten av trappan från övervåningen är en fantasifull skapelse med vikingamotiv, kanske guden Tor, samt tomtar. Den andra står i det före detta rökrummet som nu kallas vikingarummet. Här ligger också bokhandeln och kaffestugan. Auditoriet är en tillbyggnad från 1983. Runt taket löper en fris, en skämtsam och autentisk skildring av emigrantens liv med lokala inslag. Den målades på plats hösten 1983 av dalmålaren Bengt Engman från Vansbro (1925-1987).

Vagnslidret användes som garage, komplett med en vändskiva så att man slapp backa ut längs den långa uppfartsvägen. Denna byggnad används nu som kontor och arkiv/bibliotek.